Man the Aviator

Formation flying during the inter-war years.

Man the Aviator

Wing-Commander
E. W. Anderson OBE DFC

PRIORY PRESS LIMITED

Social History of Science Library

Man the Astronomer Patrick Moore
Man the Explorer G. R. Crone
Man the Industrialist Peter Hobday
Man the Navigator E. W. Anderson
Man the Toolmaker Michael Grey
Man and Measurement Keith Ellis
Man the Shipbuilder Maurice Griffiths
Man and the Wheel D. S. Benson
Man the Homemaker David Money
Man and Money Keith Ellis
Man the Builder John Harvey
Man the Farmer Robert Trow-Smith
Man the Messenger Edwin Packer
Man the Timekeeper Brian Hellyer
Man the Healer W. R. Trotter
Man the Aviator E. W. Anderson
Man and the Steam Engine G. Watkins and R. A. Buchanan
Man the Bridgebuilder Michael Overman
Man the Chemist Trevor I. Williams
Man and the Atom J. K. Thomson

84 -1424

This book is humbly dedicated to Charles Harvard Gibbs Smith the greatest living authority on the History of Aviation whose works have been read with admiration

SBN 85078 134 5
Copyright © 1975 by E. W. Anderson
Second impression 1977
First published in 1975
by Priory Press Ltd
49 Lansdowne Place, Hove, East Sussex BN3 1HF

Text set in 11/13 pt Photon Baskerville, printed by photolithography and bound in Great Britain at The Pitman Press, Bath

Contents

1 The Intrepid Aeronauts. *A cloud in a bag, life belts, down-hill towards the aeroplane, aeronautics and the people.* 7

2 Enter the Pilot. *First flyers, before the storm, the "aces," the pilot.* 23

3 Finding the Way. *From romance to realism, imperfect peace, the holocaust, pathfinders.* 43

4 Decline and Fall. *Seven formative years, the jet age, auto-mation, leaping into the ocean.* 67

5 Completing the Circle. *The new glory, pastimes.* 85

Glossary 92

Date Chart 94

Further Reading 95

Picture Credits 95

Index 96

Above. An old woodcut illustrating the story
of Icarus and his father Daedalus. They tried
to fly with wings made from feathers glued
together with wax.

1: *The Intrepid Aeronauts*

Deep within us all lies a longing to fly. This longing has been with man since the dawn of history, for the wonder and the mystery of flight is interwoven into the oldest religions. Gods are visualized as having wings or as being surrounded by winged angels. Early religious paintings show seraphims and cherubims floating among the clouds. Today, small children find it easy to believe in fairies and to dream that they too can fly, like Peter Pan.

The ability to fly has always been linked with power, not necessarily for good. Dragons and demons had wings and witches could travel through the air on broom sticks. Warriors used to wear feathered head-dresses and the great military nations, the Romans and more recently the Germans, had the eagle as their symbol of military might.

The longing to fly like a bird has lured many brave men and women to their deaths. Winged flight by man has a tragic history. Its disasters have even been woven into the fabric of fables. Greek mythology, for example, tells how Icarus escaped from prison with wings made from feathers fixed together by wax. He flew too near the sun, the wax melted, and he fell to his death in the sea.

Early scientists also believed that, one day, man would fly by his own power alone. The great philosopher Roger Bacon (c.1214–92) thought that this could be done by sitting "in the midst of an instrument turning an engine by which the wings, being artificially composed, may beat the air." Leonardo da Vinci (1452–1519), artist, mathematician and inventor actually designed a flying machine with flapping wings.

In the 1680s, Borelli (1608–79), an Italian professor, proved that the muscles of a man's arms were too weak to support his weight in the air. Nevertheless, for yet another century heroic people fitted wings to their arms and jumped off cliffs and

Below. An attempt to fly like the birds. Here, the wings are attached to the shoulders and ankles. Such inventions have always proved unsuccessful.

towers and crashed to the ground often with fatal results.

Today we accept that flapping flight using man's unaided arms is as dead as the dodo—a bird with woefully inadequate wings.

A Cloud in a Bag

Less than two hundred years ago and quite suddenly man discovered how to float in the air. In the early 1780s, the Montgolfier brothers, Joseph (1740–1810) and Jacques (1745–99), who were paper manufacturers, were throwing their bags into a pile of burning wool and straw. They were intrigued to see them rise up in the smoke. They concluded that they had found a powerful, if somewhat smelly, lighter-than-air gas. They set to work and made a linen model of a balloon about thirty-five feet in diameter which, on 5th January, 1783, rose into the air at Annonay and came down one and a half miles away.

News of this astonishing event soon reached Paris. Here the great French physicist Professor Charles (1746–1823) assumed that their success was due to the use of hydrogen. He set the Robert brothers to work at once and on 27th August launched a model that rose three thousand feet above the Champs de Mars. The ascent was witnessed by the great American, Benjamin Franklin (1706–90). "What's the use of it?" mocked a spectator and Franklin replied, "What's the use of a new born baby?"

Meanwhile the Montgolfier brothers had come to Paris and on 19th September a cock, a sheep and a duck were airborne at Versailles. On 15th October, Pilâtre de Rozier (1754–85), a doctor from Metz, went up in a tethered hot air balloon. The race to be the first to float through the air was on.

A little over a month later, on 21st November, de Rozier and the Marquis d'Arlandes, an infantry officer, went up from the Chateau de la Muette. Their paper balloon, *Montgolfière*, was a sphere about forty feet across with a large hole in the bottom around which ran a gallery for the crew. For take off, the bag had been suspended between masts and a fire lit below.

To provide extra lift during the voyage, as the air in the balloon cooled, a brazier was hung in the open neck which the

crew in the galley could stoke through a porthole. Not surprisingly, the fabric started to smoulder but de Rozier, who had specially brought with him a bucket of water and a sponge, managed to put out the fire. Twenty-five minutes after take-off, the two men landed safely after covering five and a half miles across Paris. Aviation had begun.

Ten days later, Professor Charles and Marie-Noel Robert were airborne in the *Charlière* which they had filled with hydrogen. This truly remarkable craft had almost all the features of a modern balloon. The basket or "chariot" was supported by a net over the gas bag. This bag was made of rubberized material and had an opening at the bottom to allow for any expansion of the hydrogen caused by the heat of the sun. At the top was a valve worked by a cord so that the crew could let out gas if their craft should go too high. If the balloon drifted too low they could lighten it by throwing out ballast. A barometer was provided to measure height. The *Charlière*

Above. The ascent of the *Montgolfière* in 1783 carrying Pilâtre de Rozier and the Marquis d'Arlandes. It travelled five and a half miles across Paris and heralded the beginning of aviation.

9

covered twenty-seven miles from Paris to d'Hedouville.

The hot air "cloud in the bag" became the first craft to float through the air. The following year, the first woman aeronaut, Madame Thible, the wife of a wax worker, went up over Lyons with a well-known painter in a balloon named *Gustave*. Later that year, a Scotsman, James Tytler (1747–1805) built a hot air copy of the *Montgolfière*, and made the first ascent in Great Britain, climbing 350 feet above Edinburgh.

However, the hot air balloon was to go out of fashion. Unlike the hydrogen balloon it needed a windless day for the launch or the furnace would set the edges of the fabric alight. De Rozier, seeking to obtain the best features of both types, set out in 1785 with a friend in a hydrogen balloon carrying a brazier below. Over Boulogne, the highly inflammable gas caught fire and the two brave men plunged to their deaths. They were the first aeronauts to die in an air accident.

In the nineteenth century, the hot air balloon was used mainly by the showmen. It was cheap to inflate and, with luck, would come down close to the fairground. In particular it was useful for parachuting displays. In 1849, it was used for a more sinister purpose. Carrying explosives and fitted with clockwork timers, a number of hot air balloons were launched by the Austrians against Venice. This was the first air raid in history, but it did little damage.

Although the hot air balloon had virtually disappeared, the hydrogen gas bag went from strength to strength. The first balloon flight in England used hydrogen for lift. In 1784, an

Below. The chariot of one of the early balloons showing how much equipment was carried even though the balloonists always wanted to go as high as possible.

Italian diplomat floated from London to Ware, with a dog, a cat and a pigeon as companions. Soon afterwards, Jean Blanchard (1753–1809), a Frenchman, accompanied by an American physician, made the first meteorological flight and, early in the next year, the two men set out to cross the English Channel in a balloon fitted with oars. Halfway across the balloon began to lose height and they only managed to reach the French coast by throwing everything possible overboard including the oars, a bottle of fine brandy and Blanchard's trousers.

In 1793, Blanchard gave demonstrations at Philadelphia before President George Washington (1732–99), which did much to introduce ballooning into the United States.

In the early days, ballooning was a gay social affair. The gas bags were brightly coloured and often fantastically decorated: there were pictures of gods and goddesses, signs of the zodiac, mottos, coats-of-arms. Indeed, the early balloonist was part scientist and part dandy. Although he wanted to obtain the last ounce of lift from his lighter than air gas bag, he nevertheless decorated the "shallop" with heavy draperies and festooned the rigging with flags. In addition he usually carried a massive mariners barometer mounted in a highly ornamental brass-banded teakwood case.

Right. A chariot just before ascent.

Below. Model of a balloon designed for
Napoleon Bonaparte to honour his vic-
tories. Napoleon himself was a keen sup-
porter of ballooning and used observation
balloons in 1793 at the Battle of Fleury.

The sport was so spectacular that very soon it was invaded by
a circus element. Ascents were made in a wonderful variety of
craft. One performer ascended on the back of a stag. Blanchard
himself was killed taking part in an "aerial spectacle," and in
1819 his beautiful widow died when a roman candle ignited her
hydrogen balloon as she floated above the crowded Paris streets.

In the first half of the nineteenth century balloons were
vehicles for wild adventures. In 1824, the inventor of a double
acting release valve pulled the wrong cord and was compelled to
jump out to lighten his craft and save his actress companion. In
1843, a French boy was carried aloft by an anchor that fixed
itself into the seat of his pants but fortunately he survived.

In those days, when a balloon burst, it was common practice
to let the shattered bag float into the net and act as a parachute.
This idea seems to have been suggested by an accident that took
place very early in ballooning when two men and their ballast
fell out of a basket at launch. A small boy who had been left
behind in the balloon was carried up at such speed that the bag
burst, filling the net and gently depositing the child in a nearby
river.

Throughout these years, the original *Charlière* balloon had
been improved only in detail. In 1821, cheap coal gas was used in
place of expensive hydrogen and the trail rope was introduced to
let the basket drift low over the countryside at a constant height.

Above. A balloon being dragged over the ground by high winds. To prevent this happening most balloons were fitted with rip panels to spill the gas on landing.

However, increases in the numbers of houses, and the appearance of telegraph wires on poles, tended to discourage its use.

Most gas bags were fifty feet in diameter and were fitted with "rip panels" to spill the gas on landing. This saved the basket from being towed over the ground at high speed in a strong wind. Bags of sand were carried as ballast and a grapnel was used for landing. Remarkable flights were made in such balloons. In 1836, two Englishmen covered 480 miles from London to Warburg, a record that stood for seventy years.

The gas filled balloon, like its hot air rival, was used in war. In 1789, only six years after the *Charlière* had first flown, the French army established a balloon corps. At the Battle of Fleury in 1793 Napoleon (1769–1821) used tethered balloons for observation. But the military experts of those days had little faith in such craft since they could neither identify enemy uniforms nor could they capture prisoners and interrogate them.

The use of observation balloons seems to have lapsed until the American civil war (1862–5). In 1863, freelance aeronauts were employed to observe the movements of the Confederates. These observation balloons could transmit to the ground by telegraph wires. However, the Union army became jealous and the project was eventually stopped. Free balloons made a more successful military appearance seven years later in the Franco-

Above. A balloon being dragged over the ground by high winds. To prevent this happening most balloons were fitted with rip panels to spill the gas on landing.

Prussian war (1870–1), when nearly seven hundred flights were made out of beleaguered Paris carrying passengers and mail. Replies to the letters were duly sent back by pigeon.

In World War I tethered balloons were used to report on the results of artillery fire. These military balloons were sausage shaped to lessen air resistance. Fins were added for further stability. But the tracer bullet, with its incendiary head, took a heavy toll of the inflammable gas bags. Observing also became a suicide mission for the rip cord of the observer's parachute was attached to the basket. This exposed him to attack by enemy fighters as he floated down from his flaming balloon.

Between the two World Wars (1918–1939) manned balloons virtually disappeared except for special record attempts. In 1931, Professor Auguste Piccard (1884–1962) went up nine and a half miles. Four years later two Americans rose fourteen miles above South Dakota. But distance records had largely lapsed after the German *Berliner* had travelled 1,890 miles in 1914. It

Right. Tethered observation balloon in use in the 1870s. Flags are being used to signal the position of the enemy.

had become obvious that success was only a matter of size of gas bag and endurance of crew.

For journeys by balloon, the aeronauts always tried to avoid having to leak the precious gas. But whatever precautions they took, the open neck gave off gas when the heat of the sun on the bag caused expansion. So the balloonist tried to release the correct amount of ballast to keep at the right height. A balloon weighs a good deal, and once it starts to go up or down, it is difficult to stop. Yet a couple of handfuls of sand released at the start of a downwards drift may, after a couple of minutes, change this into a climb. Since the ups can be caused by the craft passing over a town or the sun shining on the bag, and the downs can result from either a cloud covering the sun or the presence of water below, the maintenance of height by ballast needed plenty of skill.

The balloonists themselves also learned certain facts, some of which are familiar to many of us today. For example, they found that despite their great height above the ground, they felt no giddiness. This was because there were no vertical cliffs or walls to lead the eye down to dizzy depths. When the crews spoke among themselves they found that the absence of echo made their words sound thin and flat. They were also able to hear sounds coming from the ground with extraordinary clarity and to identify the sources of those sounds with remarkable ease. This was because the basket did not move in the air and there was no breeze to impair their hearing.

Part of the appeal of ballooning arose from its danger, yet the early aeronauts were well aware that a mistake could lead to a sudden and terrible death. They quickly learned that their safety depended on unceasing vigilance.

Above. The ascent in 1874 of two balloonists Sivel and Croce-Spinelli, who went up to 21,000 feet. They are breathing through oxygen bags.

Below. A model based on Leonardo da Vinci's design for a parachute.

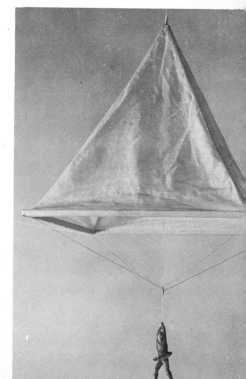

Life Belts

Parachutes have already been mentioned in connection with balloons. The original idea has been attributed to Leonardo da Vinci, who proposed a device with a pyramidical shape. But the papers he wrote had not come to light when, in 1785, Blanchard released a dog attached to a kind of large ribbed parasol.

A VIEW OF MONS^R GARNERIN'S BALLOON AND PARACHUTE

By which he ascended from the Volunteers Ground, North Audley Street, Grosvenor Square. Sep^t. 21. 1802. to the haight of 8000 Feet.
And the Parachute he descended by in a Field near St Pancras Church, quite safe.

Twelve years later, André Garnerin (1769–1823), a most courageous Frenchman, dropped by parachute from below a balloon floating over Paris. His wife, who happened to be the first female balloon pilot, followed suit two years later.

The early parachutes tended to swing wildly from side to side as the air spilled out from under the edges of the canopy. Indeed, the "penduluming" was so violent that, in England, descents were forbidden for a time. The problem was solved by making a hole in the top of the parachute. This directed the air out centrally. It then became possible to descend without becoming dreadfully sick.

The early parachutist went up in a basket hung below a balloon and then cut himself free, hoping afterwards to recover the gas bag. Indeed, not until 1908 was a parachute made that could be opened by a falling airman. In World War I (1914–18), rip cords were attached to the baskets of observation balloons and the free type of parachute was not used. In World War II (1939–45), however, free fall parachutes were used by all airmen.

Downhill towards the Aeroplane

Flying fish, flying foxes and lemurs have learned to glide. But, the soaring birds are the great experts and primitive man must have envied the gulls as they floated through the air, motionless except for the occasional tilt of a wing. The Chinese made models of birds and kept them stationary in the wind with lines, thereby inventing the kite three thousand years ago.

The earliest record of an attempt to imitate soaring birds occurs in the seventeenth century when an Italian nobleman is said to have flown at Perugia. In 1742, the Marquis de Bacqueville fitted wings to himself and leapt from a high window overlooking the River Seine in Paris. He fell onto a washerwoman's barge and was lucky to escape with only a broken leg.

The real glider pioneer appeared at the end of the eighteenth century. He was a portly British squire named Sir George Cayley (1773–1857) who carefully studied the flight of birds and made

Opposite. André Garnerin parachuting down from his balloon over London in 1802.

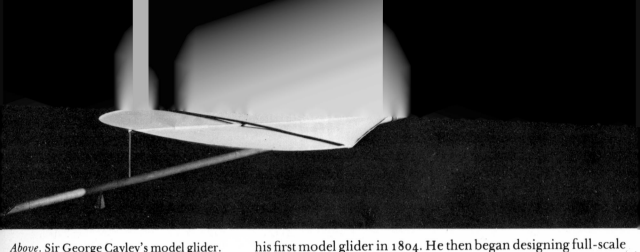

Above. Sir George Cayley's model glider. Note the upwards tilt of the wings which allows the glider to level itself. Cayley's experiments led directly to the appearance of fixed wing aircraft.

Below. One of the last flights of Otto Lilienthal, whose "hang-gliders" were a great step forward in aviation. Control was achieved by swinging the body forwards, backwards or sideways.

his first model glider in 1804. He then began designing full-scale aeroplanes. He published the results of his early tests in 1809 and his work made it certain that fixed wing aircraft would appear rather than flapping wing ornithopters. He is rightly known as the "father of the aeroplane."

Cayley's gliders were successful because they had inherent stability and were able to level themselves. This was achieved by giving the wings and the tail plane an upwards tilt. At the time, Cayley's pioneering work was overshadowed by the development of railway technology between 1830 and 1840. As a result the importance of full experiment and the advantages of inherent stability were for a time forgotten.

Towards the end of the nineteenth century, a notable advance in the philosophy of gliding appeared. Otto Lilienthal (1848–96), a brilliant German engineer, invented the "hang-glider," a small and relatively stable aircraft with a tail. The pilot was suspended by his arms and exerted slight control over his craft by swinging his body forwards and backwards or from side to side.

From 1891 until his tragic death gliding in 1896, Lilienthal built and flew a large number of gliders, biplanes and monoplanes. No wonder that the highest honour that can be won in gliding today is named after this pioneer. Percy Pilcher (1866–99), a marine engineering lecturer at Glasgow University, followed his lead and built hang-gliders until he too was killed three years later.

At the turn of the century, two brothers were building a quite novel type of glider which they were to fly at Kitty Hawk in the United States. At the time, their work was virtually unknown. The names of these brothers were Orville (1871–1948) and Wilbur (1867–1912) Wright.

Cayley had shown how natural stability could produce a safe glider. Lilienthal had proved that an aircraft could be controlled somewhat crudely by shifting the weight. The Wright brothers, who paid great tribute to Cayley's work, made the great step forward. They showed that it was possible to exert complete

control fore and aft with elevators, to correct rolling from side to side by warping the wings, and to steer straight ahead or to one side with a rudder.

The two brothers appreciated that the inclusion of natural stability was bound to make the aircraft sluggish and slow to respond. So they decided to build a glider which was *not* inherently stable so that it would respond to the slightest movements of elevator, wing warping and rudder. Just as Cayley had built the first aircraft that flew, so the Wright brothers were the first men to make an aircraft that could be flown.

Above. A view from above of one of Otto Lilienthal's "hang-gliders."

Below. Percy Pilcher flying one of his own "hang-gliders," which were based on Lilienthal's designs.

Aeronautics and the People

We have mentioned some of the remarkable men and women who pioneered flying before the invention of the aeroplane. They were a peculiar mixture of idealists with a vision of the future, sportsmen taking up a challenge, and exhibitionists seeking notoriety. A new type of man, the engineer, was now appearing.

Success had come slowly and painfully. Many of the greatest intellects, including Leonardo da Vinci, failed to realize that their ideas could only be developed by experiment. The introduction of the balloon had emphasized the value of making models and during the nineteenth century aviation gradually emerged as a science. As Lord Kelvin (1824–1907) pointed out, science is measurement; only when we can measure something do we know anything useful about it.

The 1800s saw the development in many countries of scientific societies where the science of aviation could be discussed. In 1863, the Société d'Aviation was formed in France and, three years later, the Aeronautical Society (now the Royal Aeronautical Society) appeared in England.

These scientific societies were followed by sporting clubs, the Aero Club de France in 1898 and shortly afterwards the Aero Club, later renamed the Royal Aero Club. The latter was inaugurated in a balloon. Perhaps as a result, there was a renaissance in the sport of ballooning in England until 1909, when the aeroplane captured the imagination of the world.

Yet what was the outlook of the ordinary man and woman? By 1900, the wing flappers had been hopelessly discredited. The great glider protagonists, Otto Lilienthal and Percy Pilcher, had been killed. Airships, or dirigible balloons as they were called, were only just beginning to be noticed. Free balloons and parachutes were simply regarded as display material but tethered balloons were known to be useful to soldiers. Lord Kelvin, in a famous letter to Robert Baden-Powell in 1896, summed up the situation: "I have not the smallest molecule of faith in aerial navigation other than ballooning."

The night that had descended on the heavier-than-air machine seemed to be at its blackest. Yet a number of threads were waiting to be linked together. The automobile was creating a reservoir of amateur and professional mechanics. The airships and the works of writers such as Jules Verne (1828–1905) were lifting the minds of people to the skies. Everything waited for the dawn that was to break in the west.

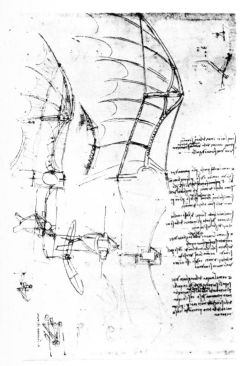

Below. Leonardo da Vinci's sketches for a flapping wing glider.

Above. A balloon race in England in 1908.
Ballooning was very popular in England and
France until 1909, when aircraft started to at-
tract greater interest.

Below. The high speed petrol engine, invented by Gottlieb Daimler, which Karl Wölfert installed in his airship. It drove Wölfert's craft at nine m.p.h.

2: *Enter The Pilot*

From the very first, balloonists attempted to propel their gas bags about the skies. Not only did Blanchard carry oars for the first crossing of the English Channel, but he also took with him a little hand driven four-bladed fan which he called a *"moulinet"* or little mill, the idea having been suggested by the blades of a windmill rotating in the breeze.

A spherical balloon sets up a good deal of resistance to motion in any direction and so a streamlined bag was suggested, in the very early days, as the most suitable shape. But the real problem was the lack of a suitable propulsion system. The rotating steam engine had appeared but it was so heavy that it made installation in a lighter-than-air craft a difficult problem.

Ingenious Frenchmen persevered, and in 1854 Henri Giffard (1825–82) flew the first airship with a cigar-shaped gas bag powered by steam, but because the engine was so small it could only drive the craft at about five miles an hour. In effect, his airship was little more than a power assisted balloon.

By 1883, the French were starting to fit electric motors to dirigibles and, a year later, they flew the first practical airship. Built for the French army, it was 125 feet long but its motor was less than nine horsepower, this craft, named *La France,* succeeded in completing a circular journey, which showed that it was not entirely at the mercy of the winds.

Meanwhile the gas engine had been invented and was used to power an experimental airship in 1878. However, it was the later development by Gottlieb Daimler (1834–1900), in 1884, of the high speed petrol engine that revolutionized propulsion. Four years later, this type of motor was installed by Karl Wölfert in a German craft which flew at nine miles an hour.

In the field of dirigibles, the Germans were now beginning to rival the French. The English were nowhere in the race. Mechanical vehicles were not allowed on British highways before the turn of the century. The effect on engine development in this country was disastrous.

In 1900, Count Zeppelin (1838–1917), flew the first of his great craft. It combined nine separate gas bags or balloonets in a 420 foot rigid envelope, with an aluminium framework. The craft was launched from a floating dock in Lake Constance in Germany so that the long and cumbersome envelope could be headed into the wind. Initially, the airship was found to be hopelessly underpowered and the visionary project ran into difficulties. For instance, with a non-rigid airship, the crew pulled a rip panel on landing to prevent the wind from dragging it over the ground. But, in contrast, a rigid envelope had to be manhandled by a large ground crew and held until it could be battened down.

Meanwhile, Santos Dumont (1873–1932), a Brazilian living in Paris, was gaily flying his little non-rigid dirigibles, descending safely in the most remarkable places, such as the top of a tall building and in a Boulevarde for a cup of coffee. As early as 1901, this colourful aeronaut completed a circuit of the Eiffel Tower.

Two years later, the Lebaudy brothers, Paul and Pierre, who were sugar refiners, at last produced a properly controlled airship. It was nicknamed *Jaune* because of its yellow gas bag. This craft completed the first true air journey in history, covering the thirty-eight miles from Moisson to Paris. Thus France produced not only the first balloon but also the first true airship.

In 1908, a giant Zeppelin was destroyed in an accident. Nevertheless, the Germans pressed ahead with this original design, and it proved so successful that they hardly altered it for the next twenty years. Between 1910 and 1914, five of these airships, each about five hundred feet long and with a speed of over thirty-five miles an hour, carried 35,000 passengers and flew some 17,000 miles without a single fatality. These magnificent flights, coupled with the increasing military might of Germany gave warning of what was to come.

In 1915, Zeppelins bombed London and other cities. But the

Below. The first true airship. Pierre and Paul Lebaudy's craft, nicknamed *Jaune*, which flew thirty-eight miles from Moisson to Paris in 1902.

giant airships were vulnerable to anti-aircraft gun fire and to incendiary "tracer" bullets. Although the crews operated with
extraordinary courage in highly inflammable craft, their losses
were too great and the raids were discontinued.

The British tried to copy the Germans. They built a large rigid
airship in 1911, aptly naming it the *Mayfly*—she was destroyed on
the ground before she flew. But by the end of the war, Britain had
started building her own Zeppelin-type craft. They were over six
hundred feet long, had five engines, and were able to travel at

Above. The Brazilian, Santos Dumont, flying
his non-rigid dirigible in 1901.

around sixty miles an hour.

The year after the war ended, one of these monsters, the *R34* made a double crossing of the Atlantic, luckily only encountering moderate winds. Then, for the next nine years, disaster followed disaster. The British *R38* collapsed in the air in 1921. Two years later the ex-German Zeppelin, renamed *Dixmude*, crashed into the Mediterranean. In 1925, the United States' dirigible *Shenandoah* broke up in mid-air.

At the end of the 1920s, the hopes of the supporters of the airship were raised by the appearance of the *Graf Zeppelin*. 776 feet long, she carried twenty passengers and over a ton of mail for six thousand miles at seventy miles an hour. In 1929, she completed a round the world voyage starting with seven thousand miles non-stop from Friedrichshafen in Germany to Tokyo in Japan. By 1937, when she was withdrawn from service, she had flown over thirteen thousand passengers and covered more than a million miles, which included a hundred and forty crossings of the Atlantic.

However, there were further disasters. In 1930, the *R101* crashed at Beauvais, France, with a great loss of life and the public outcry led the British government to end all work on airships. Later in the same year, the United States *Akron* disappeared in the Atlantic during a storm. In 1935, another American dirigible *Macon* dived into the sea and sank. Two years later came the final catastrophe, the new German Zeppelin *Hindenburg* burst into flames when mooring at Lakehurst, U.S.A.

By 1940, the airship had been virtually abandoned. Only a few small non-rigid dirigibles were left to fly around the sky carrying advertising material.

Below. The famous airship, *Graf Zeppelin*, which flew at seventy m.p.h. and completed a round the world voyage. It was taken out of service in 1937 by which time it had carried over 13,000 passengers.

The First Flyers

We have seen that airships were originally driven by steam; a similar pattern was followed in the development of the aeroplane. In 1842, William Henson, a Somerset lace maker, patented his famous *Aerial Steam Carriage* complete with twin propellors, rudder, elevator and tricycle undercarriage but the model only flew downhill. Nevertheless, Europeans continued to pin their hopes on the steam power that was driving their beloved railways. A Frenchman, Clement Ader (1841–1925), made a machine that, in 1890, hopped into the air before the admiring gaze of three witnesses and a couple of gardeners. Sir Hiram Maxim (1840–1916), an American who invented the machine gun, built a giant three and a half ton craft, but it never flew.

Samuel Langley (1834–1906), an American astronomer, made some excellent flying models including one driven by a petrol engine. In 1903, his full sized aircraft, which he called *aerodromes*, were twice catapulted from the top of a houseboat across the River Potomac, U.S.A., but each time the aircraft went straight into the water.

All these craft were based on models with inherent stability. Hence the full scale aeroplanes, even had they become airborne could not have been steered.

However, by 1902, the Wright brothers had perfected their fully controllable glider and had flown it nearly a thousand times in winds up to thirty five miles an hour.

Below. Sir Hiram Maxim's aircraft on its runway in 1894. The idea was extremely ambitious, but the aeroplane weighed three and a half tons and never flew.

Above. The Wrights testing their glider at Kitty Hawk in 1902. Orville is flying and Wilbur steadying the right hand wing tip.

Below. The only photograph of the first flight by the Wright brothers' *Flyer No. 1* in 1903. It flew for twelve seconds and covered forty yards against the wind.

Wilbur Wright was thirty-six years old and his brother Orville was thirty-two. They were bicycle makers, the sons of a protestant bishop and lived at Dayton, Ohio. After the success of their final glider trials in the sand dunes at Kitty Hawk, North Carolina, they went back to Dayton to build an engine and to design propellors. The engine was water cooled and had fuel injection; it is said to have been built by a mechanic in six weeks using only three machine tools. The two specially made propellers were driven by chains and the machine used a large number of bicycle parts.

By December 1903, the brothers were at the Kill Devil Hills with their *Flyer No. 1*. It had the usual Wright glider arrangement—a biplane with an elevator ahead, a rudder aft and wing warping for control in roll. The wing span was about forty feet and the weight less than seven hundredweight, of which the engine complete with fuel and water accounted for about two hundred pounds. The two chain-driven propellers were mounted just aft of the wings.

17th December dawned with strong winds and frozen puddles on the ground. The rail was set for take-off into the teeth of a twenty-five mile an hour wind. Four other men and a small boy

were watching when, at 10.35 a.m., with Orville at the controls, and Wilbur steadying one wing tip, the engine was run up and opened out.

After a short forty foot run, the aeroplane took off at just over thirty miles an hour and flew for twelve seconds. But it only covered forty yards against the wind. That morning three more flights were made, the last covering nearly three hundred yards in about a minute. The flight ended when the aircraft, kept deliberately close to the ground to avoid accidents, touched down accidentally in the gusty wind.

For their 1904 flying, a Dayton banker lent them a ninety acre field known as Huffman Prairie. At the first opportunity they arranged a demonstration. About fifty spectators assembled including about a dozen local reporters. Alas, the wind on the great day was only four miles an hour which the brothers knew was inadequate for take-off. However, they felt compelled to put up some sort of a display, but the engine became temperamental and the *Flyer* failed to fly. Next day they tried again, but only managed a feeble hop into the air.

Throughout 1904 and up to October 1905, the Wrights continued to fly at Huffman Prairie. At the end of 1905, in their *Flyer No. 3*, they were travelling at forty miles an hour and covering tens of miles, distance being limited only by petrol tankage. They had solved a number of problems including correct banking during turns, and now had a thoroughly practical aeroplane. As yet, the rest of the world knew nothing of the achievements of the Wright brothers.

In April 1903, a close friend of the Wright's, Octavé Chanute

Above. Front view of the *Flyer No. 1.* You can clearly see the bent wings, the elevator and the two propellers which were mounted just behind the wings.

Left. The engine of the *Flyer No. 1*, which used a large number of bicycle parts. It is said to have been built in only six weeks.

Above. The Wright biplane *No. 3* in flight towards the end of 1905. Having failed to interest the British and American Governments in their aeroplane, the Wrights did not do any flying between 1905 and 1908.

Below. Wilbur Wright triumphantly flying around the Statue of Liberty in 1909. France, rather than America, was the first country to appreciate the Wrights' success in achieving controlled flight.

(1832–1910), lectured to the Aero Club de France on the gliders built by the brothers and mentioned that their intention was to build a powered aeroplane. The reaction of the French was immediate. How could the homeland of Montgolfièr permit powered flight to be achieved first in a foreign land?

The French immediately built three copies of the Wrights' aeroplane but failed to reproduce the controls properly and all three were utter failures. They had heard about the demonstration at Huffman Prairie; surely the claims of the Wright brothers were false?—so the belief spread to the rest of Europe. The Americans were likewise disenchanted particularly because the newspapers compared what had happened at the ill-fated demonstration to the triumphs of Santos Dumont in his airship which, to them, was just another Flyer, except that it flew.

The results were very sad. By the end of 1905, the efforts of the Wrights' to interest the American, British and French governments had failed and the brothers were disillusioned. Between October 1905 and May 1908, they did no more flying. Meanwhile, Europe set to work in the wrong direction by following the false trail of inherent stability.

European airmen were basically chauffeurs, who assumed that flight depended only on power, and believed the aeroplane was no more than an automobile with wings. They saw no difficulty in driving such a craft through the air. They did not appreciate that pilots must know how to exercise complete control over the aeroplane. As a result, the aeroplanes that they might have built never materialized.

For the next two or three years, Europeans could do no more

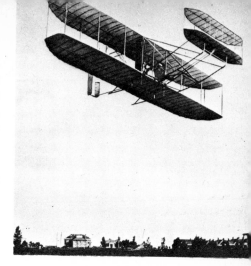

than leap briefly into the air, a notable example being the irrepressible Santos Dumont, who built an aircraft with its tail in front which hopped to universal applause. By the end of 1907, the best that Europe could manage was a thousand yard flight by a French aircraft driven by Henri Farman (1874–1958).

Fortunately, in 1908, the Wright brothers were persuaded to give a demonstration of their aeroplane in France. The two men converted their *Flyer* into a two seater and, in August, they began a series of flights at a race course near Le Mans. The flights were an outstanding triumph. The brothers were congratulated by everyone on their success in achieving controlled flight. Even the French praised the Wrights; as one Frenchman remarked: *"Nous sommes battus. Nous n'existons pas."*

In 1908, the Wright brothers made well over a hundred successful flights in Europe carrying a variety of passengers. The next year, demonstrations were given in the United States. The brothers made a further two hundred flights, carrying royalty, training pupils, and continually setting up new records which were broken time and again by themselves.

Above. Orville Wright demonstrating the capabilities of his aeroplane for the U.S. Army in 1908.

Before the Storm

Below. Wilbur Wright showing King Alphonso of Spain the layout of their two-seater biplane which had such a success at Le Mans in 1908.

The enthusiasm of the French to match the Wrights' achievement enabled them to set up new records. In 1909 £1,000 was offered by Lord Northcliffe of the *Daily Mail* for the first crossing of the English Channel. In July, a French biplane set out but came down with engine trouble. The pilot was picked up sitting on his craft nonchalently smoking a cigarette, presenting a picture of heroic calm that was subsequently to be copied by other airmen who descended accidentally into the waves.

Meanwhile, Louis Bleriot (1872–1936), an erstwhile specialist in motor-car headlamps, was preparing his small monoplane. It had a wing span of only 25 feet and an all-up weight of about 600 pounds and his 25 horsepower engine could drive his aircraft at just over 40 miles an hour.

On 25th July, 1908, in the cold grey dawn with the dew still on the ground and his trusty mechanic pointing the way to England, Bleriot ran up his engine and took off with full power, just clearing a line of telegraph wires. He soon passed over a

Above. Louis Bleriot approaching the English coast during his flight across the English Channel on 25th July, 1908, which won him Lord Northcliffe's prize of £1,000.

Below. A poster advertising an air display at Reims in 1909. At Reims, in the previous year, aircraft had been on sale to the public for the first time.

200.000ᶠ de PRIX

GRANDE SEMAINE

D'AVIATION DE LA REIMS DU 22 AU 29 AOÛT 1909 CHAMPAGNE

French destroyer which had been sent out to monitor the flight and, if necessary, to pick Bleriot up out of the water. He flew on for a few minutes and then looked back. The destroyer had disappeared in the mist and he could not see the coast of England ahead. Needless to say, he had no compass.

There was only one thing that Bleriot could do—leave his aeroplane to fly itself and hope. It would be extraordinary if the little monoplane were to carry on straight for the coast of England—but that is exactly what happened. He found himself close to the white cliffs of Dover and chose an opening between them. As he flew over the grass he cut the engine and landed safely. Immediately, some soldiers, a policeman and two Frenchmen arrived, closely followed by a customs officer, who insisted on going through the full rigmarole required to clear a yacht.

Balloons had floated across the Channel quite often in the past. Airships had managed the flight from France when the winds were not unduly adverse. But, the first crossing by an aeroplane was seen to have a special significance as it had been achieved irrespective of winds. To the British the message was clear. It was no longer sufficient for an island nation to claim that it "ruled the waves;" now it also had to command the air.

Soon after Bleriot's crossing, the first Air Display was held at Reims in France. Eighteen flights were recorded, six by American aircraft and twelve by the French. In addition, aircraft were on sale for the first time in public.

During the next two years, the French went from strength to strength. The Baroness de Laroche was the first woman to qualify as a pilot. Other Bleriot monoplanes crossed the Channel, one even carrying a passenger, "Miss Paris", a buxom tabby cat. Bleriot machines were in great demand although there was a feeling that the single wing, even though strutted and fitted with bracing wires, must be a source of weakness.

Bleriot soon answered his critics. Early in 1913, he had taught a young man named Pégoud to fly and finding him a born pilot used him to test his aircraft. In September of that year, Pégoud demonstrated the strength of the single wing by performing various aerobatics.

By the end of 1913, French aeroplanes held the world records for distance, height and speed. Their engines powered all British and many American aeroplanes. To this day, the golden age of French aviation is remembered by the large number of Gallic words in world wide use such as fuselage (aeroplane body), nacelle (engine casing) and aileron.

Soon, the rest of Europe, alarmed by the prospect of war, was catching up fast. Most of the aeroplanes built were biplanes.

Those with propellers in front of the engine were known as "tractors" and those with propellers behind as "pushers." One advantage of the former was that, in the event of a crash, the pilot would fall onto the engine rather than the engine onto the pilot.

In the ten years following the flights at Kill Devil Hills, aviation had made great progress. Aeroplanes had begun to carry mail. Seaplanes fitted with floats had landed and taken off from water. Landings on ships had taken place. The invention of radio had made it possible for pilots to talk to those on the ground. National air forces had been formed and trained in reconnaissance and in directing artillery by "spotting" the fall of shells. In Russia, Igor Sikorsky (1889–1972) was building multi-engined transports to match the German Zeppelins. The Italians had dropped large grenades on protesting Turks. Europe, under the pressure of imminent war, had overtaken the Americans.

In July and August 1914, the nations drifted into World War I. Orville Wright was to comment wryly, "When my brother and I built and flew the first man carrying flying machine, we thought that we were introducing into the world an invention which would make further wars practically impossible."

Above. The public inspecting a Bleriot monoplane at Hendon aerodrome in 1911. Many thought the single wing must be a source of weakness despite the bracing wires.

The "Aces"

Most people in Europe were about to go on their summer holidays when World War I broke out. If they were surprised, it

Above. During the early days of World War I reconnaissance aircraft carried observers armed with rifles to fire at the enemy.

was fortunate that their governments were not. The Germans had about two hundred "first line" or combat aircraft with a number of other machines in reserve for training and other purposes. Many of these aircraft were monoplanes, such as the Taube of Austrian origin and the Fokker, designed by a Dutchman but built in Germany. The Germans also had twenty or so Zeppelins.

The French, too, were well prepared, with something approaching a hundred and fifty aircraft, mostly biplanes though a few monoplanes were included. The English had rather more than fifty aeroplanes, all biplanes fitted with French engines. Thus the English and French roughly matched the Germans, but the Germans had bigger and faster machines. The Italians and the Russians had relatively few aircraft and the Americans, who were not to enter the war for a couple of years, had only twenty aeroplanes, including trainers, on their total strength.

The admirals realized the value of airships and aeroplanes for following the movements of enemy warships but the generals has little faith in aviation. Ferdinand Foch (1851–1929), later to become the Allied commander-in-chief, had commented that flying was "good sport but, for the army, useless." The cavalry, in particular, objected to the noise of the aeroplanes which tended to frighten their horses. Nevertheless, aeroplanes were used for reconnaissance and to "spot" the results of artillery fire. Radio was used to pass back information to the gunners.

In the beginning two-seater aircraft were mainly used. The pilot flew the machine and another man acted as the observer.

Above. The method of dropping bombs on the enemy during World War I.

The aeroplanes used were roughly the same wingspan as the original Wright Flyers, but had engines of up to a hundred horsepower. They were able to travel at around eighty miles an hour and fly as high as two miles or ten thousand feet. Enough petrol was carried to stay aloft for several hours. In addition, there were single-seater scouts, the absence of the observer making possible the fitting of a larger engine and therefore higher performance.

Reconnaissance aircraft attacked enemy troops by dropping iron darts or hand grenades. The ground troops, in reply, used machine guns and artillery converted to fire into the air. Rifles and pistols were originally carried by the observers to fire at enemy aircraft, but rifles were awkward to handle and were quickly abandoned. Pistols were replaced by light machine-guns.

At the beginning of the war, the advantage lay with the two-seater pusher biplane, in which the observer sat up front with a machine gun and a grandstand view all round. The single-seaters were faster and had no trouble in escaping if they saw the two-seaters in time, but they had no means of taking any offensive action.

The French tried to solve the problem by a device which would let the scout fire ahead through its propellor. But they failed to solve the technical difficulties. In 1915, one of their pilots fitted metal plates to his propellor blades so that he could fire at enemy aircraft while he steered at them. He was shot down over the German lines while bombing a train. Antony Fokker

(1890–1939), who saw the device, set to work to design an interrupter gear to make sure that the machine-gun would fire only into the spaces between the revolving blades.

By the end of 1915, the new Fokker aeroplanes were wreaking havoc among the Allied aircraft. The advantage of a high performance single-seater (from which everything possible was stripped) with a gun platform of extreme steadiness, was overwhelming. The Fokker could come up behind a pusher two-seater and shoot it down without any fear of retaliation. Only the few tractor biplanes with an observer in the rear cockpit had a good chance of surviving. Thus for the first time, but by no means the last, a single invention was to transfer superiority in the air battle to one side.

The French fitted machine-guns to the top wings of their biplanes but, in this position, the guns could neither be reloaded nor cleared if they became jammed. The British scouts

Below. The perfect attacking position. Here, the attacker is diving down on his enemy out of the sun.

Above. The Fairey F2A, an early long-range aircraft.

were provided with guns in the fuselage that pointed outwards so that they would miss the propellers. The small two-seater pushers were converted into scouts with a single gun at the front. By 1916, the Allied aircraft were beginning to get on equal terms but, early in the following year, the new improved German fighters swept the board. However, in the summer of 1917, the long awaited high performance Allied scouts, with twin belt-fed machine guns firing ahead through mechanical interrupter gear, gained a superiority that was to last until the fighting ended.

In combat, the object was to attack from above and with the sun behind, in the hope that the enemy fighter would not see its adversary in time. If the first pass was not successful, the diving attacker found himself ahead of his adversary and in a similarly vulnerable position. In the subsequent *melée*, every effort was made to get on the tail of an enemy aircraft, and shoot him down. In reply, the aeroplane ahead turned as sharply as possible in the hope of getting behind his attacker. Combat then became a matter of aircraft circling behind each other, the one with the tighter turning ability eventually coming up astern of the other. In such a situation, to dive away would be almost certainly fatal because it temporarily presented the other fighter with a steady target.

The introduction of the incendiary tracer bullet, at first intended to let the fighter pilot see where his shots were going so that he could make the necessary deflection, meant that often an aircraft would become a "flamer." Yet, although a few German aircraft were fitted with parachutes, these were denied to British and American airmen. This was partly due to the extraordinary

Above. Baron Manfred von Richthofen, better known as the Red Baron, in front of his aeroplane. He was perhaps the finest air ace of World War I.

theory that parachutes might encourage pilots to desert their aircraft before it was strictly necessary but it was also part of the dreadful disregard for human life shown by the generals in World War I.

In order to attack out of the sun, the fighter had to be able to climb high and quickly. To turn inside an adversary and get onto his tail, the aeroplane had to be extremely manoeuvrable. And so performance became more and more important and aerobatics—originally little more than features of air displays—became part of the stock-in-trade of the fighter pilot. Max Immelman (1890–1916) invented a special method of turning sharply which enabled him to come up behind his attacker. This tactic was named after him by both sides.

The German pilots began to operate in groups or "circusses," one of the most famous being led by Baron Manfred von Richthofen (1882–1918) who was known as the Red Baron owing to the colour of his aeroplane. The Allies followed suit and formation flying was conceived. During World War I battles, in which over a hundred aircraft were involved, occurred in the skies over Flanders.

From these combats, there emerged certain outstanding individuals, who had the skill to close with their targets almost to collision point, and an uncanny ability to allow in their aiming for the sideways motions of their adversaries. These men were the "aces" and were the heroes of the day, better known than most generals and respected by both sides.

The peculiar isolation of air battles from the gruesome war on the land and its emphasis on skill as well as courage, tended to inculcate a mutual respect between the pilots of both sides. They had no animosity towards their enemies and often felt pity and remorse when an aircraft was seen to fall in flames. These young men were gallant in the true sense, and their combats took on some of the flavour of jousting tournaments in days of old.

These pilots could only fight if their flying was instinctive and so they tended to identify themselves with the aircraft in which they were operating. Indeed they only survived by that peculiar skill which made them integral parts of their machines.

By the end of the war, fighter aircraft were flying nearly five miles up and could climb the first two miles in ten minutes. Their speeds, low down, were about a hundred and fifty miles an hour, but they could travel much faster in an attacking dive.

As the pilot's skill improved, so did aircraft design. Towards the end of the war, after a tussle with the German authorities, Hugo Junkers (1859–1935) built a monoplane of iron and steel instead of wood and fabric. Its single wing was built on the cantilever principle and had no struts on supports. It was also mounted low so that, in a crash, some of the shock would be absorbed. This revolutionary design was to influence the whole future of the aeroplane even though it came too late to affect the outcome of World War I.

In 1917, the Germans brought into service the first long range bombers, the Gothas, which operated against London by day and by night. These aircraft flew at sixty miles an hour and each carried a ton of bombs. By the end of the war, Handley Page was building four-engined aeroplanes with a speed of ninety miles an hour, a range of two and a half thousand miles and a bomb load of three and a half tons. The war ended before these aircraft had the opportunity of attacking Berlin.

Anti-aircraft defences against the bombers consisted of guns and, at night, searchlights. The former could only put up a "barrage" or curtain of shrapnel. This type of shelling was similar to an artillery bombardment and families living near London were forced to take their children downstairs in case shrapnel penetrated their houses. At night, searchlights might pick up and "cone" a Zeppelin and then the guns had a chance to shoot it down. But such defensive measures were relatively in-

effective against the Gothas. Nevertheless, few people built shelters and indeed they often watched daylight raids without any concern for their safety. Even so, air raids generated powerful emotions and gave a sinister connotation to aircraft in general.

Towards the end of the war, a profound change in air policy was beginning to emerge. Aircraft were now being used not only to help armies and navies, but also to bomb aircraft sheds, airfields and railways. Comparatively little damage was done but the signs were there. Accordingly, in 1918, the British army and navy air forces were merged into one Royal Air Force able to take on these new and basic tasks.

The aeroplane had served the Army well and had ended up by being used to attack ground troops. It had also been of use to the navy. One aircraft had sunk a Turkish battleship by dropping a torpedo—an action which upset the British Admiralty who had always claimed the impotence of flying machines in the face of naval armour.

When war ended, the British had about three and a half thousand front line aircraft, sixty times the number with which they had started in 1914. Nearly all were fitted with British engines. The French aeroplanes had multiplied by a factor of about thirty but the German aircraft, which suffered heavy losses towards the end of the war, had only increased by a factor of about twelve. Nothing is known of the Russians except that, just before the October Revolution in 1917, they were building a thousand aircraft a year.

Below. The cockpit of a V.C. 10. Note the "half-spectacles" of the control column, which works on exactly the same principle as that of the earlier control sticks.

The Pilot

The advent of the aeroplane added a new dimension to aviation. The balloonist altered his height by letting out gas or by dropping ballast, but he could only go where the wind took him. The airship aeronaut reached his destination by steering his craft like an aerial chauffeur. However, the pilot of an aeroplane changed height and direction at will by altering the attitude of his craft, that is, the angle at which it was driven through the air.

To control attitude, the pilot initially had a stick between his knees. Tilting the stick forwards or backwards would make the elevators push the nose of the aircraft down or up; tilting it sideways would bank the aircraft towards the side that the stick was moved. The same principles applied when the stick was later replaced by a control column with a half-wheel or "spectacles" at the top. Pushing the column forwards or backwards made the nose of the aeroplane fall or rise. Turning the wheel caused the aircraft to bank to one side.

The pilot's feet rested on a rudder bar mounted on a central axle and connected to the rudder by tiller lines. *Pushing* the right hand side of the bar pulled the right hand tiller line and turned the rudder—and the aeroplane—to the right. Unfortunately, most people learn to ride bicycles in which, to turn to the right, the right handlebar has to be *pulled*. However, the "crossed" rudder bar has been perpetuated in the two rudder pedals of a modern aircraft.

To keep his aircraft level or to alter its path, the pilot had not only to co-ordinate a number of actions properly but also to remember the attitude of his machine. In the air, there is no ground nearby and the instinctive sense of level is disturbed by accelerations, particularly those that occur in turns. Until instruments were provided to help him, the pilot had to learn the tricks of compensating for errors in his sensations. This was known as "flying by the seat of the pants."

For landing, the aircraft had to descend towards the near edge of the airfield while flying into the wind so as to travel as slowly as possible. But if the aircraft approached the airfield too slowly the airflow over the wings would be upset and the craft would "stall". Early on the pilot learned to feel when he was going fast

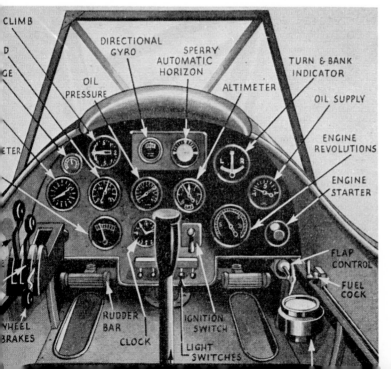

Left. The diagram shows the controls used by pilots in the 1940s. The crossed rudder bar and the control stick are the same as in earlier aircraft, but instruments such as the air speed indicator and the altimeter only came much later.

enough by the wind on his face. Later, an "airspeed indicator" was fitted so that, provided he did not let the reading fall below a certain minimum value, he would know that his aeroplane would not stall.

Before take-off it was necessary to make last minute checks. The stick and rudder bar were tested to make sure the elevators, ailerons and rudder were working. The engine was run up to test out the twin ignition systems, each one being switched off in turn. His tests made, the pilot would push open the throttle and hold it there knowing that, unless he were travelling fast enough, the trees ahead at the edge of the airfield would not be cleared. He was also aware that a change of mind might be fatal. Thus the pilot learned to be simple minded and to take decisions and stick to them.

In this new world there was nobody that the pilot could blame for his mistakes. To keep alive, he had to be vividly aware of all that was happening around him. He had to take decisions that, even if not ideal, were not basically wrong. He tended to solve problems, not by weighing factors, but by choosing the dominant feature, and acting as if it alone existed.

Thus man the aviator grew from an aeronaut into a pilot and entered into a world of danger and beauty. To survive, he had to be simple as well as accurate. Perhaps he found it hard to express his hopes and fears to those about him. As Wilbur Wright once said, "the only bird that talks is the parrot and he don't fly very high."

Below. A French artist's impression, in the 1920s, of the likely effects of aviation in the year 2000. Although it is a spoof, it does reflect the great enthusiasm for aviation that developed after World War I.

3: *Finding The Way*

The progress in aircraft design since 1914 would have taken many decades to complete in peace time. In World War I it did not matter if an expensive experimental aeroplane crashed on its first flight since the nation footed the bill. Of what significance was the death of yet another brave man when so many hundreds of thousands were being slaughtered in the mud of Flanders? Thus the aviation industry had been cushioned by war against many of the problems of development. Maximum effort was concentrated on improving performance in battle, irrespective of cost.

We see now that, when the war was over, the time was ripe for great adventure. The pilots were experienced and the aeroplanes were good enough to establish new records. But, by 1918, the basic conception on which aviation was founded had been forgotten.

A hundred years earlier, Cayley had written of the great "navigable ocean of the air" with routes open at all times to all places. As a countryman familiar with the early problems of the railways he saw the aeroplane as a means of travel irrespective of intervening woods, hills, rivers and lakes. Together with other air pioneers, he looked upwards at the freedom of the skies. But, the miracle of flight had been so dazzling that it had blinded aviation to the importance of navigational aids.

Fortunately, the newpapers were to provide the catalyst. The prize awarded to Louis Bleriot by the *Daily Mail* has already been mentioned and William Randolph Hearst (1863–1951), the American newspaper owner, had encouraged flying in the United States by offers such as $50,000 for a flight between the Atlantic and the Pacific coasts. Lord Northcliffe (1865–1922) now put forward £10,000 for the first non-stop crossing of the Atlantic by an aeroplane.

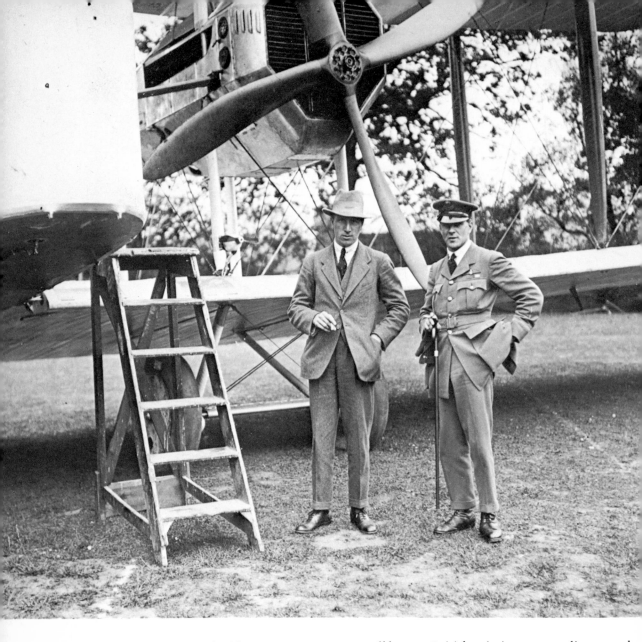

Above. John Alcock and Arthur Brown beside their aeroplane—a converted Vickers bomber. In 1919 these two British airmen made the first non-stop crossing of the Atlantic.

In May 1919, a well known British aviation personality named Hawker set out with his friend Grieve from Newfoundland in a single-engined aircraft. Less than half-way across, the aeroplane came down in the Atlantic Ocean. A thorough search found neither survivor nor wreckage and hope was abandoned. Messages of sympathy were sent to their relatives from Buckingham Palace. Meanwhile, the two men were travelling home on the good ship *Mary*, a small Danish vessel with no radio, beside which they had landed in the sea. Everybody went wild with delight and the men were given a remarkable welcome when eventually they reached London.

During this dramatic interlude, John Alcock (1892–1919) and his navigator Arthur Brown (1886–1948) were getting ready in

Newfoundland. The aircraft was a converted twin-engined Vickers bomber with a 67 foot wing span, designed to fly at 100 miles an hour, or at 70 miles an hour on one engine. The total weight was five tons of which three tons was made up of fuel.

This was not the first flight on which a pilot had carried a navigator. For overwater journeys, the intrepid aviator would be joined by a mariner who, armed with a compass wrapped in a box of cotton wool, guided the pilot to his destination. But it was almost certainly the first long flight that was carefully prepared navigationally. The aeroplane carried three compasses and Brown had a naval sextant and a system of transparencies that enabled him to convert star observations into a position on his chart.

It was evening in Newfoundland but 4.30 p.m. in London when on 14th June, 1919, the heavily laden bomber climbed into the sky. By nightfall, the aircraft was flying between layers of cloud which opened for brief intervals to allow Brown to check his position by the stars. Their height was four thousand feet and there was a tail wind. Although the radio generator had broken down, all was proceeding according to plan.

Just as dawn was breaking the aeroplane flew into a thick bank of turbulent cloud. Snow, rain and sleet beat on the fuselage and ice covered the airspeed indicator inlet so that it no longer gave a warning of a stall. For a short time, the aircraft was uncontrollable and lost height rapidly until Alcock caught a glimpse of the sea. He managed to level off just above the wave tops.

Luckily the sudden descent had unfrozen the airspeed indicator and the aircraft was climbed to six thousand feet, still in appalling weather. More cloud necessitated a further climb and at this point, ice began to appear on the leading edges of the wings.

Ice, too, was forming on the engine air intakes and the motors were beginning to lose power. There was only one answer. Brown undid his safety belt, took off his gauntlets, and in the freezing rain clambered out into the slipstream roaring over the slippery wing to hack away with a knife at the ice forming just behind the spinning propeller. Brown went out onto the wings six times before Alcock risked bringing the aircraft down low over the water. The dangerous descent was made without loss of control and at three hundred feet it was possible to see ahead under the clouds.

The two men flew on into the daylight without seeing the sun or a passing vessel, and hearing nothing on their radio receiver. Then, at 8.30 a.m., a dark patch on the horizon resolved itself into land and the masts of Clifden radio station, on the west coast of Ireland, appeared out of the murk. Thankfully, Alcock brought the aeroplane down onto a large green meadow and the machine upended itself onto its nose. They had covered nearly two thousand miles at an average speed of almost two miles a minute and the prize was theirs.

In 1922, it was the turn of the Americans. Lieutenant James Doolittle, (1896–   ) who later became a famous general, made the first coast to coast flight from Florida to San Diego in a day, a distance of nearly twenty-two hundred miles. Two years later, four United States amphibian aircraft circumnavigated the world from Seattle in the U.S.A. via Japan, India, Europe, Iceland and Greenland.

However, one flight was to overshadow all the others. In 1927, a prize of $25,000 was offered by a rich American of French origin for the first direct flight between New York and Paris. Two Frenchmen set out from Paris in May and were never heard of again. Shortly afterwards, Charles Lindbergh (1902–74) set course from New York in his little single-engined monoplane, *The Spirit of St. Louis*. Its wingspan was only forty-six feet.

The flight was meticulously planned but hardly any navigational aids were carried except a new type of magnetic compass. The first twenty hours were a harrowing experience, for Lindbergh was completely unable to check his position. He could only hope his course was correct. Lindbergh afterwards

Below. Charles Lindbergh's *Spirit of St. Louis* in which he made the first solo non-stop crossing of the Atlantic in May 1927.

recalled that, when at last he saw ahead the coast of Ireland, he realized that he was still a land animal.

As soon as the *Spirit of St. Louis* was sighted over Ireland crowds began to gather at Le Bourget, the Paris airport, and, as further news came of the progress of the flight, the excitement grew. Perhaps 150,000 people saw the little monoplane come in after covering the 3,600 miles in less than thirty-three hours, and the crowds completely swamped the official reception. Lindbergh then flew to London where he was given the same rapturous welcome.

Lindbergh became an international hero overnight and, although other record breaking flights of importance followed, none received the same amount of acclamation. To everybody this trans-atlantic flight seemed to be the ultimate achievement in aviation. Lindbergh's reaction was to vow that never again would he undertake a long flight without some form of navigational aid.

Around the time of Lindbergh's solo effort, light aeroplanes began to appear in numbers in the United States, Germany and England. One of the most famous was the De Havilland "Moth," a compact little British biplane with a cruising speed of ninety miles an hour. In 1930, the twenty-two year old Amy Johnson (1903–41) flew one of these aeroplanes from England to Australia. Twelve thousand miles in nineteen days!

Below. Amy Johnson in her De Havilland "Moth" just before her England to Cape Town flight in 1932.

Above. The De Havilland "Moth." Both Amy Johnson and Francis Chichester flew this type of aircraft on their pioneering flights.

It was in a Moth that Francis Chichester (1901–72), later to become a world renowned yachtsman, flew from New Zealand to Australia. His little aeroplane had only enough fuel to reach Australia by putting down half-way at Norfolk Island, a tiny strip of land in the middle of the shark-infested Tasman Sea.

Before take-off, Francis Chichester calculated the angle above the horizon at which the sun would be at different times throughout the day as seen at Norfolk Island. Then he set out flying and taking sextant observations of the sun in his relatively unstable little biplane until the angle was correct for Norfolk Island. He turned and continued flying, observing and altering course in the intervals so as to keep the sun always at the calculated angle until he came over his objective and landed.

This was the end of the golden age of aviation when men and women flew because they liked flying. Their machines were not the heavy bricks of the modern age but light and frisky craft that responded to the touch as if they were alive. There was fun as well as technical achievement in their voyages through the uncharted oceans of the air.

From Romance to Realism

For a long time converted warplanes were used by civil aviation. In February 1919, the Germans began flying between Leipzig, Berlin and the new seat of government at Weimar and the French opened a Paris to London run. In August, the British inaugurated the first daily schedule, carrying a dozen passengers between London and Paris in two and a half hours. The Dutch airline K.L.M. started the same year and the rest of Europe followed soon after.

In addition to passengers, mail was carried and was indeed much preferred by the airline operators. As one French airline official explained, if an aircraft carrying nothing but mail were to crash, it was too bad but, if there should be passengers on board, endless tiresome questions would be asked by the relatives. Indeed, although a regular air service was set up between Florida and Cuba, internal passenger carrying was not to start in the United States for many years.

The American post office was sending mail by air before the war ended. The performance of the aeroplanes was adequate

and the pilots were highly skilled, but navigation was sorely neglected. There were no weather reports, no deicing equipment and no instruments for blind flying. Three out of every four of the pilots, who originally operated the mail service, lost their lives. But, by early 1921, the situation had improved and,

Above. The first daily passenger service to Paris in August 1919. The trip usually took two and a half hours.

in the U.S.A., letters were travelling regularly between New York and San Francisco in less than a day and a half.

By 1927, mail shuttles were well established in America and a freight service was operating between Detroit and Chicago. Aircraft such as the Lockheed *Vega*, which could carry six passengers for nine hundred miles at 135 miles an hour, were now available. Civil aviation began in the United States and grew very rapidly.

Most of the new aeroplanes had single pilot crews. To help the pilot navigate, loop aerials were fitted which would point in the direction of a radio transmission. At all the big airfields, radio beacons were set up so that the pilot had only to tune into the right frequency and fly with his loop pointing ahead to reach his destination. On arrival, the loop would switch from pointing dead ahead to indicating astern.

Below. A direction finding loop aerial in the flying boat *Caledonia* in 1937. It relied on radio transmissions from the radio beacons sited in the big airfields and was a great help to navigation.

By 1929, the radio range had appeared in the United States. A ground station transmitted morse dots from one fixed loop and morse dashes from another. From the four diagonal directions or "beams," the dots and dashes would intermingle, causing steady signals in the pilot's headphones. If the pilot deviated from the beam he only heard dots or dashes. A chain of weather stations reported when conditions were likely to be too bad for flying. Thus, with a catalogue of beams and their frequencies, it was a simple matter to fly from one radio range station to the next across the north American continent.

In the early 1930s, the new generation of German and Dutch three-engined transports appeared, carrying nearly twenty passengers at over two miles a minute. In the United States, they were followed by twin-engined all metal monoplanes complete with retractable undercarriages, deicing equipment and flaps to reduce stalling speed. The most famous of these was the Douglas

Above. The Douglas D.C.3, or *Dakota*, the most popular transport aircraft of the 1930s.

DC3, later to be known as the Dakota, which carried 21 passengers at 170 miles an hour for 500 miles. It was still flying forty years later.

During the 1930s, flying became an accepted form of travel in the United States but, in Europe, it still retained some of its aura of glamour. On disembarking, passengers tended to swagger very slightly and, if they met their pilot, they would thank him profusely. A journey by air still had the flavour of adventure.

Imperfect Peace

The formation of Britain's independent Royal Air Force was an experiment watched with interest by other nations. People were not willing to allow military expansion in the glorious years of peace. Therefore the new service had to appropriate funds previously ascribed to armies or navies. Thus the Royal Air Force found itself sandwiched between powerful and politically experienced generals and admirals.

At the end of the war, Britain was given a mandate to administer Iraq. In 1921, insurrections broke out in the mandated territory. It had always proved difficult to deal with rebels by using troops, as the British Army had found to its cost in India. The sight of soldiers setting out to make war on their own countrymen would inflame local sentiment, and running battles had to be fought all the way to and from the disaffected areas.

The proposal put forward by Lord Trenchard (1873–1956), the head of the new Royal Air Force, was as follows. Should a village refuse to obey the local administration, aircraft would drop leaflets to warn the people that, unless they submitted to law and order, their houses would be bombed. If intransigence went on, the villagers would be told that, on a certain day, explosives would be dropped on their houses. By this method, the daily life of a dissident village could be disrupted and the rebel villagers brought to heel with no loss of life. The policy was extraordinarily successful and the cost to the British nation very small. The Royal Air Force had made itself a viable force in its own right.

Luck continued to follow the new service. In 1925, the Schneider trophy, a race against the clock over a closed circuit for seaplanes, had been won by the great Doolittle. In 1927, the British built a special aeroplane, the Supermarine that pushed up the speed to two hundred and eighty-two miles an hour. Similar Supermarine monoplanes carried off the next two contests, raising the speed to six miles a minute and winning the trophy for Britain. The last of these aircraft later set up a world speed record of over four hundred miles an hour.

These successes raised little interest at the time, for a race amongst seaplanes seemed to have nothing to do with people's desire to improve their standard of living. As a result, the building of monoplanes with their special engines was very nearly stopped by the British government. The problem was solved by the generosity of the patriotic Lady Houston who supported the venture with large sums of money. Partly as a result of her help, a new generation of high-speed fighter monoplanes was developed in the 1930s and the Royal Air Force was able to start the World War II equipped with Spitfires and Hurricanes.

Below. A replica of the Supermarine monoplane which won the Schneider Trophy for Great Britain in 1927.

In the United States, the four-engined Flying Fortress made its debut as early as 1935. It was designed to act as long-range artillery for the U.S. Army and was armed with multiple machine-guns so that it could battle its way through to targets. The American fighter aircraft were less progressive, perhaps because the air defence of their nation seemed a problem of little urgency. On the other hand, the threat of Japanese air power and aircraft carriers had accelerated work on naval strike aircraft.

By the treaty signed at the end of World War I, Germany was forbidden to built military aircraft. In the early 1920s, the prohibition was being undermined by training pilots on gliders and by building factories far bigger than were needed for a civil aviation programme. By 1930, Adolf Hitler had begun to ignore the treaty, and in 1935 it was known that the German Luftwaffe had a strength equal to that of the Royal Air Force. By the beginning of World War II, the Germans had twice as many aeroplanes as the British.

From the British independent air force two significant policies emerged. Lord Trenchard had continually preached the doctrine that wars could be won by strategic bombing and new four-engined bombers were on the drawing boards. Even more

Below. A diagram showing the way radar operates. The British fighter defence radar system proved invaluable to this country during the Battle of Britain.

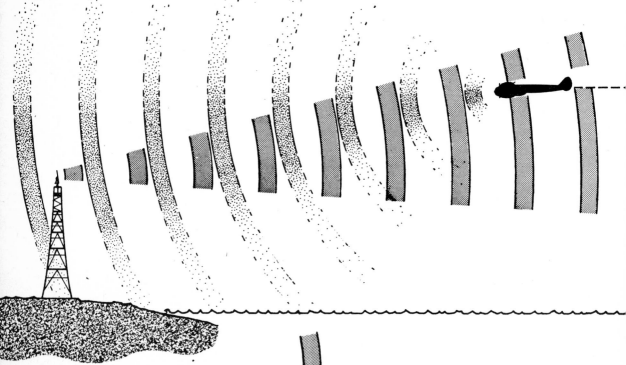

BEAMED PULSES FROM TRANSMITTER

PULSES REFLECTED BACK TO TRANSMITTER BY AIRCRAFT

significantly, his prognostications had also stressed the need for strategic defence.

By 1939, a new fighter defence system using radar had been developed by Watson Watt (1892–1973). Radar was purely an element, though a vital one, in an overall system which had been scientifically studied. The major problems were those of identifying aircraft, tracking of enemy aeroplanes and vectoring defending fighters towards them.

The Holocaust

Within a minute of the British declaration of war in 1939, the air raid sirens were sounding in London. People filed down to their shelters, mentally congratulating the Germans on the promptness of their reaction. It was a false alarm and so were many of the rest of the warnings during 1939 and the early part of 1940. Indeed, this period was known as the "phoney war."

In May 1940, the Germans launched their great offensive against the French and English armies. They began by invading Holland, with whom they had a long record of peaceful relations and, to settle matters quickly, they destoyed the centre of Rotterdam by air attack. In the next few weeks, France was driven out of the war and the British army only just managed to escape across the Channel from Dunkirk.

During this disaster, the independent Royal Air Force, ignoring criticism from the army, held back. Thus, although the Army was temporarily helpless, the air defences in terms of radar, fighter aircraft and trained pilots were unimpaired.

By June, the French were defeated, the Germans began to mass troops and aircraft along the northern coasts of France and Belgium ready to invade England. Their High Command knew they could not hope to cross the Channel until the Royal Air Force had been defeated. Unless this was done the barges carrying the troops would be exposed to attacks from the air, and from light naval forces operating under the umbrella of defensive fighters.

In August, the crucial battle for air supremacy began. The Germans had the advantage of numbers, their fighter supremacy being more than two to one. Both sides had highly

Below. Civilians sheltering in Liverpool Street Station, London, during the Blitz.

Above. A squadron of Hurricanes (with Spitfires in the background) about to intercept the German bomber formations. It was usual for the Spitfires to attack the German fighter escorts, leaving the bombers to the Hurricanes.

professional pilots and excellent machines, but the British were fighting for their lives. The Luftwaffe launched continuous attacks on airfields but the coastal radar defences prevented any surprise attacks. The fighting in the air was extremely fierce. Large forces of Spitfires and Hurricanes were directed against the German bombers. Losses on both sides were heavy and although the smaller British air force battled with extraordinary tenacity, their losses were proportionally greater. By the end of August, the Royal Air Force was on its way to defeat.

The Luftwaffe was under the control of Air Marshal Hermann Goering (1893–1946), who had succeeded Von Richthofen as the leader of the Gruppe when the Red Baron was shot down. Goering was anxious to show that he and his airmen could win the war singlehanded. Accordingly, at the end of August, he stopped attacking fighter airfields and began bombing London and other English cities.

This change of policy enabled the Royal Air Force to recover and by mid-September the lightly armed German bombers

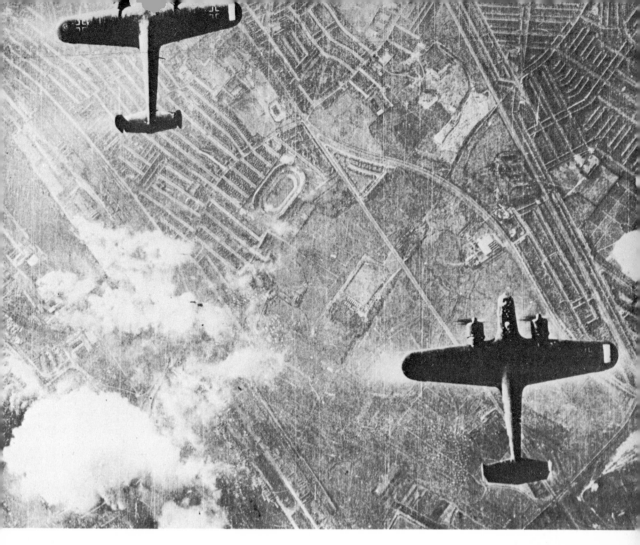

were being shot down in large numbers. By the end of the
month, the Battle of Britain was virtually over. The courage and
the stamina of the British fighter pilots against skilful and deter-
mined attackers had been supreme. As Prime Minister Winston
Churchill (1874–1965) said in the House of Commons, "Never
in the field of human conflict was so much owed by so many to
so few."

Beaten by day, the Germans began night attacks on London.
These attacks continued until the middle of 1941 by which time
the British anti-aircraft guns were being aimed by radar and
night fighters, equipped with radar, were operating against the
enemy aircraft. Finally, in June 1941, Germany invaded Russia
and the bombing attacks ceased.

The "Blitz" had caused great distress in England but the effect
on the war effort had not been great. Although the German
crews were of a high standard, they found it extremely difficult
to hit a target except on a bright moonlit night. Under these
conditions, bomber aircraft were particularly vulnerable to

Above. Two Dornier 215 bomber aircraft,
photographed from another German aircraft, over South London.

Above. Scramble! Hurricane pilots dashing for their aircraft during the Battle of Britain.

night fighters. The Germans therefore developed "beam" systems to guide their aircraft to the aiming points. However, these attacks were not always successful.

For example, in May 1941, an attack was made on the Rolls-Royce aero-engine works at Derby. Two hundred and thirty bombs and a large number of incendiaries were concentrated with great precision in open fields, the only casualties recorded being two chickens. It will be remembered that a "beam" is produced by two interlocking radio transmissions. The signals had been detected by British scientists, who thereupon added a third transmission. This caused the line of balance of the "beam" to be distorted and the bombs fell wide of their targets. A new factor was being added to warfare, conflict between scientists. The "war of the wizards" had begun.

Throughout the dark days of the Battle of Britain and the "Blitz," attacks by the Royal Air Force on Germany had been increasing. The British bombers were mostly twin-engined, carrying a crew of up to five men with the pilot as captain. Lightly armed, and vulnerable to attack by fighters, these aircraft could only operate by night. Although the crews were doing their best, they faced the same difficulties as the Germans at the start of the "Blitz" and few were dropping their loads within five miles of their aiming points.

By early 1942, the "wizards" were working hard on airborne electronics and the bomber force was gathering its strength. Work on the four-engined bombers that were to carry ten ton loads to Berlin had never ceased. In May, the first "thousand bomber" raid took place but the results, from the Allied point of view, were disappointing. However, in August, the new bombers were coming into service and a Pathfinder force was created to lead the way to the targets. The most modern equipment was channelled into this force and, by the end of the year, Pathfinder aircraft were equipped with radar. The bomb-aimer could now see the pattern of the ground below, whatever the weather conditions.

Unfortunately, the policy of British bombing had already been laid down. In the early days of the war accurate bombing had proved an impossibility. Therefore "carpet bombing" had been initiated. This meant that a heavy weight of explosive was launched into an area in the hope that the main target would be damaged or destroyed. It was also believed that this type of bombing damaged civilian morale, but it had the same effect on the Germans as it had had on the British. If homes were destroyed, people slept beside their machine tools in order to increase the output against the hated enemy.

Left. A Lancaster night bomber on her way to Germany. In August 1942 to help the bomb-aimers, the Pathfinder Force was set up. Its job was to mark the target with flares so the bombers could see what to aim for.

It must also be remembered that, until 1944, bombing had been the only major way in which Britain could attack Germany. Hence the tonnage dropped on the enemy per month became a gauge of effort. As a result, attacks were made in unsuitable weather and operations against crucial targets that demanded special aiming techniques were discouraged because the setting aside of squadrons for training meant a reduction in the dropping of tonnage. Nevertheless, some extraordinarily successful specialized attacks were made, dams were breached, canals mined and battleships sunk.

During 1942 British merchant shipping suffered great losses from German submarines. Instead of trying to protect the convoys, the Royal Air Force laid siege by air to the ports from which the submarines operated. This forced the German submarines to remain submerged throughout their criuse, which greatly reduced their operational range. Furthermore, an air attack on a submarine would come so suddenly that even if the craft survived, exploding depth charges caused multiple injuries and deaths inside the hulls.

In 1943, the American Flying Fortresses were used as daylight bombers. At first they were extremely vulnerable to German fighters. However, their losses diminished once they were provided with an "umbrella" of Allied fighters. At this stage, the Germans introduced their new rocket-propelled Komet fighters.

These extraordinary little aircraft jettisoned their undercarriages at take-off and climbed to thirty thousand feet in two and a half minutes. They then had seven minutes fuel left. They flew at 600 miles an hour and could climb up to 54,000 feet. Their armament consisted of two large cannons. After attacking the bombers they would glide down and land on a skid, but the force of the landing often caused what little was left of the fuel to explode, so that more Komets were destroyed on landing than in battle.

By the end of 1943, the night bombers were attacking Berlin. The weather was often bad and crews seldom saw their targets. Accurate bombing was a matter of aiming at the markers dropped by the Pathfinders. Over the target, the anti-aircraft "flak" was intense.

By 1944, the Germans were using their *V1* pilotless bombers which flew at four hundred miles and hour. Over the target, the burbling motor would cut out and there would be a deathly hush before the aircraft flew itself into the ground and exploded. Later, the Germans attacked London with their twelve and a half ton *V2* rockets which came down onto their targets, 220 miles from launch, at three times the speed of sound. Fortunate-

Below. The four geographical groups of Fighter Command.

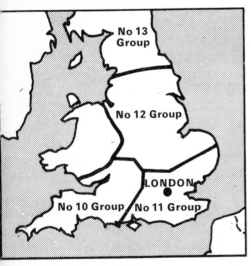

P.F.CASTLE

Above. A diagram of the Flying Bomb, or *V1* pilotless bomber, which the Germans began using in 1944.

ly, not long after the attacks began, the Allies invaded Normandy and the *V2* missile sites were over-run.

To defend their towns the Germans began to use jet fighters to attack the bomber streams. But they were introduced too late to have an appreciable effect. Around the clock bombing was now a dreadful reality. Beautiful cities such as Leipzig were laid waste almost casually. Finally, the Germans surrendered and only the Japanese fought on.

In December 1941, the Japanese air force had attacked the American fleet at anchor in Pearl Harbour. In the subsequent naval battles of the Coral Sea and Midway the American and Japanese fleets fought without firing a gun at each other, relying entirely on attacks by aircraft. As a result of these two great battles, the United States recovered command of the Pacific. From then onwards, the Americans gradually closed in on the Japanese mainland, leapfrogging from one group of islands to the next. Bombing attacks started in 1942 with a raid on Tokyo led by General Doolittle.

In 1944, the Japanese air force, in desperation, launched their

Top Right. The central part of Hiroshima immediately after the atomic bomb had exploded.
Bottom Right. The city as it is today.

Kamikasi attacks. Japanese pilots in aircraft crammed with explosives flew themselves into enemy ships. In the battle for the island of Okinawa in 1945, nearly two thousand of these suicide strikes were made, causing serious damage to the American fleet.

By August 1945, the war in Germany was over. However Japan still refused to surrender. The United States, after a series of leaflet raids to warn the inhabitants, obliterated Hiroshima and Nagasaki with two atomic bombs. Hundreds of thousands of people died or suffered from the effects of radiation. It was the most dreadful manifestation of the power of the air. The Japanese immediately capitulated and World War II was over.

What of the airmen who took part in the operations? They

were of two types, the hunters and the hunted. Pride of place among the hunters must go to the single-seater day fighter pilots who carried on the great traditions of the aces in World War I. As before, the most successful attacks were made from above and with the sun behind. The fighters, now in radio contact with each other, operated in close formations. As in World War I there was gallantry and mutual respect even in the heat of battle. These young men were the cream of the pilots in the nations at war. They will never be forgotten.

Perhaps the best example of the hunted were the night bomber crews, for their aircraft were very vulnerable to fighter attacks. One night they might listen to madrigals on the banks of the Cam and the next evening they would take off with the shadows lengthening below to bomb men, women and children that they never saw. They knew that a proportion of those setting out would not come back. They carried parachutes but, if caught by the crowds below, might be thrown into the fires they had started.

During the war, the civilian population endured the air raid warnings, the hurry to the shelters, the noise of the guns and the thumping of heavy bombs. Air raids often ended with the sight of people picking their way through piles of rubble that had once been their homes. It says much for the forgiveness of human beings that, a generation later, Europe was able to work together within the framework of a Common Market.

Pathfinders

The period between the end of World War I and the end of World War II saw pilots learning not merely to fly their aeroplanes but to direct them to the right places. To do this, they often needed the services either of a navigator in the aircraft, or of a controller on the ground.

A notable exception to the rule was civil aviation in the United States, which was reliant on radio beams. European nations were slow to copy, perhaps because their homelands were small and relatively well served by railways. Their aviation services

Above. A camera-gun film sequence of the destruction of a Messerschmitt 110 by a British fighter in World War II.

mainly formed links with dominions, colonies and protectorates, involving flights over oceans, or across countries uninterested in radio aids.

In the middle of World War II, radio systems that painted patterns over wide areas, rather like intersecting ripples on a pond, were developed by the British and the Americans. The Germans gave up their beams, but went on with a long-range dot and dash beacon system, which was neither jammed nor faked because it was so useful to Allied seamen and airmen.

All such devices pale into insignificance compared to radar which was used by ground controllers and installed in all aircraft except the single-seater day fighters. A radar system uses waves ten thousand times as long as light waves. So the picture painted by radar on a screen is far coarser than that seen by the naked eye; and it has no colour discrimination. As a result, specially trained observers had to be trained to interpret ground radars and were carried in aircraft to operate airborne systems.

Together with a radar system, aircraft were fitted with automatic pilots. For bad weather landings, the British installed "Fido," which has been described as a heaven-sent device disguised as the flames of hell. To improve visibility great jets of paraffin were lit alongside the runways to burn off the fog in the immediate vicinity.

The numbers of aircraft that operated from each field led to the development of control towers, following the pattern used in the United States. Aircraft coming in to land would be made to orbit the airfield until the ground controller in the tower

Below. A 1935 airliner alongside Croydon airport control tower, which was fitted with radio to enable the ground controller to guide each aircraft down in turn.

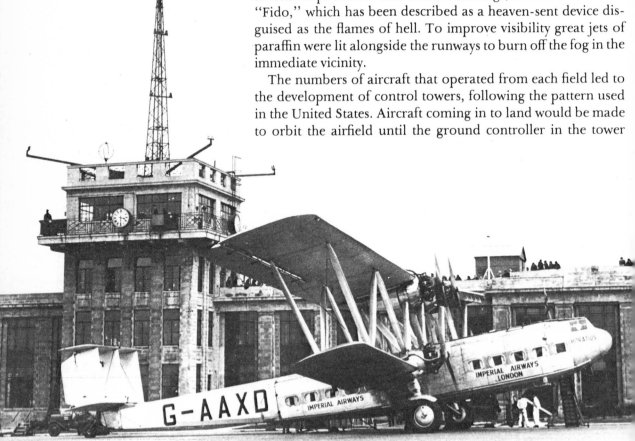

could guide each one down in turn. All these developments were to change radically the pattern of future aviation.

We have seen that the period between the two World Wars was the golden age of the aeroplane. We have shown the triumphs, mechanical, electronic and human of World War II. If aviation was to change, it could hardly change for the better.

Below. The transmitter room of one of the radar stations set up to give an early warning of attacks by German bombers.

Above. The long-range ballistic missile *Polaris*
just after firing. Because of their accuracy
and destructiveness rockets have now
replaced long-range bomber aircraft.

4: *Decline and Fall*

The dreadful consequences of the atomic fission bombs dropped at the end of World War II, and the later development of the far more powerful hydrogen bomb, transformed the face of war. Battles between powers that possess nuclear weapons are now seen to be a form of mutual suicide. Even if one nation discovers a means of deflecting the aim of enemy rockets, the fall-out from the radio-activity in the "winner's" weapons would spread right around the planet.

So long as people continue to go to war the nuclear weapon will make the victory worthless. All that we have to fear is that some lunatic Samson may one day pull down the pillars of the world, and in his blindness destroy us as well as himself.

The area of damage produced by weapons of mass destruction is so great that the old ideas of accurate attack become less valid. The long-range ballistic missile, which in two or three minutes of motor burn, steers a nuclear warhead to a geographically known target, has a range sufficient to strike anywhere in the world with an accuracy of about a thousand yards. Such accuracy is more than adequate when the area of devastation is measured in square miles. Rockets have therefore replaced the long-range bomber aircraft.

We have already seen how victory in an air battle goes to the high-performance fighter which is able to turn quicker than its adversary. The limit at which an aircraft can turn depends on how much acceleration a man can withstand before his heart becomes unable to pump blood into his eyes thus causing temporary blindness. We can help the blood get to his eyes by special clothing that discourages concentration in other parts of the body. We can also make him lie down in his cockpit so that his heart and head are roughly at the same level. Nevertheless, a point will arise at which any human being will "black out" in a prolonged high-speed turn.

Below. A Japanese soldier suffering from the effects of radiation in Hiroshima in 1945. We can now see that nuclear warfare is a form of mutual suicide.

On the other hand, a missile can be designed with an electronic eye which is virtually unaffected by accelerations. Furthermore, the missile can be fired at a seconds notice at a pre-selected target. In fact, only the defensive missile can hope to combat the incoming rocket warhead.

What then is the future role of the military airman? He is adept at recognizing patterns and taking decisions in complex circumstances. Both these abilities are needed to support armies in fluid land battles and, to a lesser extent, in naval warfare. In wars in which atomic weapons are not used the role of the airman will remain much the same. But safety against the defensive missile will probably make it necessary for the aeroplanes to operate at high speed and as close to the ground as possible.

The "colonial" wars in Korea and Vietnam have shown there is also a demand for helicopters to fight tanks, supply and reinforce troops, and rescue the wounded. At sea, helicopters search for submarines by hovering over the surface and "dunking" radar-like devices that rely on sound waves rather than radar to penetrate the water.

In addition, large slow multi-crew aircraft able to remain on patrol for long periods are used for submarine detection and attack. These are fitted with complex systems and are operated by teams of specialists working in what are virtually small operations rooms. Large aeroplanes may also be needed to carry early warning radar. For reconnaissance, the high speed aeroplane is supported by the satellite.

In short, the airman may still play a significant role. But in the event of a major nuclear conflict, the key factor will be the ingenuity and the management ability of the scientists and electronic engineers.

Seven Formative Years

At the end of World War II, European war aircraft were converted into civil transports by redesigning the interiors. Such aeroplanes tended to be uneconomical in operation but they filled the gap until custom-built aircraft could be designed and tested. It was seven years before these new aircraft came into service.

In the United States, the situation was quite different. During the war America had continued to develop and manufacture civil transport aircraft not only for her own needs but also for her allies. For example, the excellent twin-engined monoplanes of the late 1930s were improved and four-engined aircraft introduced. Thus in 1945 America was in a dominating position.

As a result, the United States played an important role in establishing the post-war policies for civil aviation. The Civil Aeronautics Board had been set up in America in 1933 and the Radio Technical Committee followed two years later. In 1944, I.C.A.O. (the International Civil Aviation Organisation) was inaugurated at Chicago. Furthermore, purely American organizations such as A.R.I.N.C. (Aeronautical Radio Incorporated) introduced standardization of aircraft equipment which spread out all over the world.

After the war a new basic short range civil aid known as V.O.R.(V.H.F. Omnidirectional Range) was introduced. This aid was coupled into the autopilot to guide the aircraft along selected paths to and from the beacons. To help an aircraft land, a special narrow beam system I.L.S. (Instrument Landing System) had been developed. With these two aids the pilot was able to navigate without difficulty over land and a specialist navigator was needed only for long oceanic flights or journeys across countries with no navigational aids.

Yet the greatest change that appeared during this formative period was in improved communication systems. In 1930, civil

Below. The Instrument Landing System in operation.

aviation pilots sometimes talked to their airline companies. By 1940, V.H.F. (Very High Frequency) communication with control towers on airfields was general. In the United States, area control centres were set up to look after aircraft, give weather reports and assist in case of distress. By 1950, an official communications system had been established and Civil aviation pilots used separate frequencies to contact the ground controllers.

In 1945, controllers of airfields were forming incoming aircraft into "stacks." Aircraft circled in orbits one above the other, the lowest being called in to land and the others stepped down in turn. By 1952, the airways were becoming dangerously congested. Aircraft travelled too fast and, when approaching head-on were too small to be seen. Furthermore, the absence of an obvious horizon allowed pilots unknowingly to focus their eyes at the "rest" distance of about six feet. So collisions occurred even in clear weather. As one pilot remarked after an accident, "it was like looking down the barrel of a rifle after the trigger had been pressed."

The airman operating along airways was forced to accept that, with the open skies all around him, he was to be cabinned and confined by ground controllers. He was no longer the master of his fate. Only on long-range flights over water could the navigator choose his own route. In the next decade, even this liberty was to be denied him. For the problem of civil aviation had changed. It was no longer a question of reaching one's destination, but of following a route predetermined by air traffic control.

To ordinary people, aviation had developed from something rather special to an accepted method of travel, particularly on the longer journeys such as across the Atlantic. The Russians had already decided to link their cities and towns by air and had built hundreds of smaller airfields. Their passenger traffic was about half that of the United States.

In Russia, Tupolev was producing new giant aircraft carrying 224 passengers for five and a half thousand miles. This huge transport was beaten for size by the *Antonov Antheus*, a colossal freighter that could lift nearly forty five tons a distance of seven thousand miles. These aircraft were planned for routes from Moscow to New York and to Tokyo.

Between 1945 and 1952 the pattern of the pilots' cockpit became standardized and is still followed today. It is based on two pilots side by side, with the captain on the left, each pilot having his own control column, rudder pedals and set of flight instruments. These are grouped below an "artificial horizon" which consists of a light sky and a dark ground, the boundary

moving up or down or tilting sideways just as the real horizon would move when compared to the nose of the aircraft.

To the left of the artificial horizon is an airspeed indicator, and to the right an altimeter that shows height above mean sea level; the compass is mounted immediately below. These four instruments thus form the "basic T" and others are placed at the

Above. The inside of one of the first airport control rooms in Britain. This primitive transmitter and receiver at Croydon airport in 1920 was a direct forerunner of the more advanced equipment that was installed after the war.

Above. The cockpit of a Trident 1 airliner. The "basic T," which includes the altimeter, airspeed indicator, artificial horizon and compass is outlined in white immediately in front of the control column.

sides on lower down. Between the two pilots is the "pedestal," which carries throttles and autopilot switches. On a panel above the engine instruments are arranged in rows so that, by glancing along each row, the pilot can see if all his engines are working at the same speeds, pressures and temperatures. Switches and radio frequency controls are generally sited in the roof.

For long overwater flights a navigator, usually sitting behind the pilots, was still carried. If the aeroplane had four engines and it was necessary to watch the performance of each, a flight engineer might be found sitting beside the navigator to monitor both the fuel intake and performance of the engines.

Increasingly important in the operation of civil aircraft was, of course, the air traffic controller. Before take-off, he would be given details of the intended route and projected times of arrival at various points along that route. This information would be updated either by position reports relayed by radio from the aircraft or by picking up the aeroplane on air traffic radar. By means of this information, the controller made sure there was adequate separation between individual aircraft and avoided

possible collisions by changing their routes or by requesting them to circle at certain points. Initially the process was somewhat haphazard and, as one air traffic controller was heard to say "our best chap is St Christopher." But gradually the system developed and mid-air collisions became very rare.

The Jet Age

Even before World War II, work had been going ahead in Germany and Great Britain on the jet engine. Ernst Heinkle (1888–1958) had flown a jet aircraft in 1939 and a Gloster, powered by a Whittle engine, was airborne in 1941. By 1945 the

Right. Sir Frank Whittle (on the right) showing a journalist one of his early jet engines.

Germans and the British were equipping fighter squadrons with the new jet-engined aircraft. The Americans and the Russians were not far behind and their jets were to tangle five years later in the Korean war (1950–1).

It had been thought that the speed of sound was the point at which an aeroplane might go into an uncontrollable spin or dive. But, in 1947, the American Bell aircraft flew at one and a half times the speed of sound, and the only result was that the air could not get out of the way sufficiently quickly, and "supersonic bangs" were produced by the shock waves.

Jet engines quickly pushed up speed and height records. By 1953, the American Skyrocket was flying at twice the speed of sound and reached a height of fifteen miles. The United States had also produced an eight-engined jet bomber. Yet the first jet transport, the British Comet, was already operating a service between London and Johannesburg, South Africa.

This forty-ton seater aeroplane cruised at nearly five hundred miles an hour at a height of seven miles. At this height, the

Below. The first jet passenger transport, the British Comet standing next to the aircraft (the D.H.108) from which it was conceived.

atmospheric pressure is less than half that at the Earth's surface. The Comet's fuselage therefore had to be pressurized by an amount equal to half the air pressure at sea level in order to keep the passengers alive.

The handful of Comets originally built were operating perfectly when one of them blew up in mid-air for no apparent reason. It was known that the pressure cabin was extremely strong and it was assumed that the disaster was due to turbulence. Then two more Comets climbed into the sky and blew up. In 1954, the fleet was withdrawn from service.

After a long enquiry, the cause was identified. The rapid climb up to six miles caused the pressurized cabin to swell and the descent to ground level for landing led the hull to contract. The weakest points in the Comet cabins were therefore being twisted to and fro like the wire that holds in the cork of a champagne bottle. The metal became fatigued and broke and, like champagne squirting out, the pressure in the cabin blew passengers and seats out of an ever increasing hole, wrecking the aeroplane which disintegrated immediately.

Shortly before the modified Comets appeared, the Russian Tupolev twin-jet aeroplane went into service. At the end of 1958, just after a new transatlantic Comet schedule had begun, the first of the new long-range four-engined American jets, the Boeing 707, followed suit. Other similar aircraft followed all of which, like the Boeing, were larger and faster than the Comet, carrying around a hundred passengers at ten miles a minute.

At about the same time as the long-range American jets were appearing, the French Sud Aviation Caravelle entered service. It was roughly the same size as the Comet and slightly faster, but it was unique in two ways. Firstly, it was the first short-range jet and secondly, its engines were mounted aft whereas all previous jet transports had engines in the wings. This design was quickly followed by manufacturers all over the world.

Below. The B.A.C. 1-11. This new airliner has the jet engines mounted aft, like the original French Sud Aviation Caravelle.

This remarkable simultaneous appearance of jet aircraft all over the world sparked off a race by airline operators to re-equip. Although the change to jet aircraft was partly emotional, it was also based on hard economics. If one aircraft flies twice as fast as another, it can do twice as many journeys and, given that the two aeroplanes have similar passenger capacity, it can carry twice as many people. In addition, speed has an appeal to passengers, particularly to those to whom "time is money."

The next stage in civil aviation development was reached in 1969 with the introduction of the first of a new generation of giant passenger-carrying aircraft known as "jumbo jets." These aeroplanes carry five hundred passengers at speeds of more than a mile every six seconds. The increase in size means that the same crew, with only a few more stewards and stewardesses, can fly a much greater number of people. Just as speed has always had economical advantage so, too, has size.

If the Jumbo jet is the move towards size, the supersonic civil transport is the move towards speed. By 1975, the supersonic airliner, represented by the Anglo-French Concorde and the very similar Tupolev, may be in service.

Supersonic transports have wings that differ greatly from the narrow swept-back design of the subsonic jets. Their wings are delta shaped so that, from below, the machines look like gigantic darts with long noses. For the low speeds involved in a landing, the wing is tilted up at a large angle. To give the pilot a better view, the nose is arranged to droop so that the aeroplane, as it comes towards the runway, looks like a huge bird peering anxiously downwards.

Early supersonic aircraft will carry a hundred or more passengers at more than twice the speed of sound; a mile will be covered every two and a half seconds. The next generation of civil aircraft will cover a mile in one and a half seconds but will need to be built of new types of metal.

With such aircraft, a problem has arisen which was not so

Below. Britain's supersonic airliner of the future, the Anglo-French Concorde, taking-off. For landing the nose of the aircraft is lowered to give the pilot a view of the runway.

noticeable in the subsonic jets. At the equator, the sun "travels" westwards at a little over one and a half times the speed of sound. Thus a supersonic transport also travelling westwards will "beat the sun" and arrive earlier in the day than when it set off.

Even in a subsonic jet, a flight which involves travelling east or west can be very tiring due to change in the local time. Suppose that we start in the morning to fly to New York. That night, when it is eleven o'clock in London, our bodies will be ready for bed. Yet it will only be six p.m. in New York and our American hosts will not want to say good night for another five hours. This alteration in the rhythm of our daily lives is known as "jet-lag."

Below. The pilot of a British Airways V.C. 1(checks his route on a map. Technology is so advanced today that the aircraft pilot is becoming a manager rather than a manipulator.

Automation

The problems of finding the way along the paths laid down by the air traffic controllers have been eased by new devices. Inertial navigation systems, which can monitor the progress of a craft by information gleaned from accelerometers and gyroscopes, were first developed to guide long-range missiles. Today, smaller and more accurate systems can be fitted into aircraft. Navigational positions can be found, irrespective of speed, with an error that increases with time at the rate of about one mile each hour. Hence the Concorde flying at 1,450 miles an hour can travel that distance with an error of only one mile.

In addition, the aircraft can be fitted with a computer which can provide a wide range of information for the pilot. As a result, even for long transoceanic flights, the specialist navigator has become redundant.

The automation that has replaced the navigator has also affected the pilot. Doolittle gave his famous exhibition of blind landing at Mitchell Field in 1929, after which the idea languished until the late 1950s, when the British invented a simple system to enable their jet bombers to be dispersed to safer airfields in the event of a sudden attack in bad weather. Yet it took ten years before automatic landing could be proved sufficiently safe to be accepted by civil aviation, and another five before it was put into regular service.

Above. An engineer officer's view of the control panel on the flight deck of a V.C.10.

To exercise proper control during a landing, an automatic system has to possess adequate power or "authority" and yet it has to be designed so that its strength will not be misapplied. Usually, three quite separate autopilots are fitted each of which has adequate authority to control the aircraft during a landing. If one of the autopilots should go wrong, its authority would be overridden by the other two. The chances of this happening during a landing has to be so remote that a second fault, or a third fault in the event of there being four autopilots, would occur on less than one in ten million landings.

With an autopilot system of this degree of reliability, it is obviously unsound to allow the pilot to interfere with it unless something has happened that the designers cannot have foreseen. For example, if the runway were obstructed by a crowd of people, the autopilot would not react but the pilot could. In fact, all he would have to do would be to open up the throttles and the automatic system would then trim the aircraft to a smooth take-off.

Thus the latest type of aircraft can be flown without using the control column, the pilot guiding the craft merely by pushing switches and twiddling knobs. Not only automatic landing, but automatic speed control, air intake and icing control systems are in use. The pilot is now becoming a manager rather than a manipulator.

A comparable development is likely to occur in air traffic control. As the number of aircraft on the routes becomes greater, the controller is able to handle only a lesser volume of air space. Aircraft will travel through the smaller sectors more quickly but they still have to be taken over from and handed back to controllers in the adjacent sectors. Thus, as traffic increases, the point will be reached at which the controller is fully occupied in communicating with adjacent controllers and has no time to handle the aircraft themselves.

To prevent situations of this sort from arising, computers are gradually being introduced on the ground. They will take much of the routine work off the shoulders of the air traffic controller and he will be left to deal with the unexpected, with the emergency that the computer cannot hope to foresee.

In addition to the computer, the air traffic controller is being given improved radar coverage to help him follow the paths of aircraft. Possibly, space satellites will give him even more information. In all this, there must be one gnawing fear. The stupidity of man, which shows itself in aircraft hijackings, could also be manifested in the sabotage of the vital air traffic control centres.

Above. A typical radar picture of an area of 200 miles radius around London. The outline of the coast of England and France has been electronically superimposed.

Leaping into the Ocean

The early aviation pioneers visualized the air as a sea that came to every man's front door. What these visionaries had not foreseen was the speed at which the aeroplanes would fly.

A modern subsonic jet transport has wings designed for travel at ten miles a minute. For take-off, the aerodynamic shape of the wings has to be altered by an adjustable "droop" at the leading edges, and by "flaps" at the trailing edges. The aeroplane needs three or four thousand yards of concrete to become airborne, and it comes in to land travelling at over a hundred miles an hour and needs a considerable distance to pull up. Some aircraft

Above. An aerial view of London airport showing just how much space an airport takes up in the middle of a city. Future airports will have to be sited further away from the centres of cities in order to cause the least possible inconvenience to city-dwellers.

even carry a parachute to be streamed behind after landing.

Furthermore, an aircraft needs to land and take-off into the wind in order to reduce the touch down and the lift-off speed and to avoid sideways strains on the undercarriage. Therefore an airport has two runways at right angles, or three runways disposed about the points of the compass with a tendency towards the prevailing wind. Since landing and take-off rates limit the capacity of an airport, there are usually double runways. Hence, with taxi tracks, unloading and loading bays, repair and maintenance shops and facilities for handling passengers and cargo, an airport which handles conventional aircraft covers a very wide area.

Air transport exists to carry people and their goods to centres of population. But people tend to congregate in large cities and airports cannot occupy large areas of land where people want to live and work. Inevitably, runways have to be sited in the suburban fringes. These are generally dormitory areas where families live. Thus the aeroplane takes-off from the runway and then climbs out over peoples' houses with its engines at full power making a great deal of noise.

It is clear that the aeroplane is in conflict with the society that it seeks to serve. It occupies large areas of valuable space in suburbs and the engine noise causes acute distress. We must therefore expect that, as urban areas grow and as air traffic builds up, new runways will have to be sited further and further away from city centres. There will be increasing demands to eliminate those airports which are the most convenient for the airline users.

The navigable ocean of the air may be everywhere but the points at which the modern transport aeroplane may enter or leave it are being removed further away from the centres of population. The airport will therefore tend more and more to be a staging post, at which people and their goods will be transferred to some form of medium or short range suburban transport, such as road, rail or perhaps a different form of aircraft.

Let us therefore now look at aircraft which do not need long runways, and which climb vertically out of small airports, thereby disturbing fewer people by noise. In 400 B.C., Chinese children were playing with toy helicopters made from a piece of stick with feathers stuck into the top, each feather being twisted slightly so that it would strike the air at an angle as the stick was spun. Probably this toy was inspired by the sycamore seed with its single wing that rotates as it descends from the tree.

A number of people prominent in aviation, including Leonardo da Vinci and George Cayley, had thought of helicopters. Many of the early ideas came from Russia, in particular from Kilbaltchitch who designed a craft lifted vertically by rockets.

Above. A model of Leonardo da Vinci's idea for a helicopter.

Probably the first man to get airborne in a helicopter was Louis Breguet (1881–1955), who as early as 1908, achieved a jump of ten or fifteen feet. Similar hops were made in Germany at about the same time. However, these craft had no more chance than the early European aeroplanes of being developed because, once again, the problem of stability had not been solved. The helicopter is quite unlike the aeroplane for it cannot be given inherent stability. If the rotor lifting up a craft should begin to tilt, and cannot be corrected by a pilot, the rotor will go on tilting until the helicopter turns upside down.

Shortly after the end of World War I, a Spanish aircraft designer, Juan Cierva (1895–1936), saw one of his aeroplanes stall on the approach to land. If a sudden loss of lift occurs at height, the pilot can recover but, if it happens low down, the accident report will read "he stalled and spun in."

By 1923, Cierva was building a new type of aircraft which he called an autogyro. It had an ordinary aircraft fuselage and

Below. Juan Cierva's autogyro which has an ordinary aircraft fuselage and uptilted wings. Despite its unconventional appearance this aircraft did not stall and crash like so many of the early helicopters.

propeller but the wings, instead of being fixed, were made like an uptilted windmill. The slipstream from the forward motion caused the blades to rotate and their shape gave the necessary lift. The slower the fuselage travelled, the less the lift, but there was no sudden stall.

By 1926, autogyros were being built in England and other countries soon followed. All types of fuselage were used and, in order to shorten the take-off run, the engine was eventually made to clutch into the rotor to start it spinning. For the next ten years autogyros were being flown all over the world, but particularly in Russia. By the end of the 1930s, the helicopter was emerging as a viable form of aircraft.

Sadly, Cierva was killed in 1936 when, as a passenger in a fixed wing aircraft, the pilot "stalled and spun in." Today the autogyro (commonly known as the gyroplane or gyrocopter) is still being built for private flying and crop dusting because it remains a remarkably cheap form of aircraft.

Although the autogyro languished, Cierva's work had brought into strong relief the problems of stability. He had shown that, if the rotor was clutched into the engine while the autogyro was airborne, the machine became unstable and the fuselage began to rotate in the opposite direction. By the end of the 1930s, helicopters were being built successfully, particularly in Germany, and one famous lady pilot, Hanna Reitsch, actually flew one indoors in a sports stadium.

In 1939, Igor Sikorsky (1889–1972), who had escaped to the United States during the Russian revolution, produced his first helicopter with a single main rotor and a small tail rotor to offset the rotation of the fuselage. Although, during World War II, helicopters were not used in quantity by Germany or by the United States, Sikorsky's work was to set the pattern for a large range of future helicopters. These machines were used with great success for rescuing wounded men and transporting troops and supplies during the Korean war, and later became part of the normal equipment of armies and navies all over the world.

Helicopters have rescued thousands of sailors at sea. They have been flown within a few feet of rock faces to lift injured mountaineers to safety. They have carried prefabricated houses to a mountain site and one has lowered a steeple onto a church tower. By the mid-fifties, they were beginning to be used for short-range passenger freight and mail, flying between main airports and smaller heliports at nearby cities.

Helicopters are ugly craft, perhaps because they are specialized, like insects, in contrast to the more graceful, general purpose, commercial aircraft. Also they are noisy because the

Below. A modern helicopter landing on an aircraft carrier. Now that most of the problems of stability have been solved the helicopter has become part of the normal equipment for armies and navies all over the world.

tips of the main rotor reaches a speed of sound and, since the forward speed is low, the noise stays with the listener for a long period.

Few airlines have operated the helicopter profitably on scheduled routes. More energy is needed to lift a load by a rotor that to pull an aeroplane wing through the air. The helicopter's rotating wing, too, is a complex piece of machinery and needs a great deal of very careful servicing since any fracture would almost certainly prove disastrous. Indeed, it has been calculated that a helicopter is economical only over routes of less than a hundred miles.

Certainly it is possible to land and take-off on a small pad but the surroundings of this pad have to be clear. The most critical part of a helicopter flight is just after take-off and just before landing. Unless the craft has sufficient forward speed, an engine failure would cause a sudden drop and the pilots would not have any autogyro effect to help him. With adequate speed, auto-rotation can be switched in and the helicopter landed safely.

But the helicopter is not the only solution to the smaller airport. Other craft which need only a short runway have been designed. In 1952, a flying platform with two fans below was used to lift a man, control being achieved, like the hang-glider, by the pilot leaning to one side to offset the tilt. In 1954, a "flying bedstead" was built in England which had two downwards-pointing jet engines for lift. Similar work was in progress in the United States.

Below. The "flying bedstead" built in 1954 in England.

By 1963, the various ideas were taking shape. The French were interested in separate engines to produce the extra lift necessary for take-off, thereby converting the conventional aircraft, with normal wings into an S.T.O.L. aeroplane (Short Take-Off and Landing). The Americans, including the Canadians and the Germans, favoured fitting jet engines to the wings and tilting the wings themselves to achieve V.T.O.L. (Vertical Take-Off and Landing). In England, the forerunner of the V.T.O.L. Harrier "jump jet" (in which the jet effluxes are deflected downwards) was being flown.

It is generally expected that S.T.O.L. airports will be able to approach closer than conventional airports to the centres of industry and population. But, because of the noise and the possibility of accidents, it is doubtful whether V.T.O.L. airports and helicopter "pads" will appear in many city centres in the next few years. Thus the original dream of the pioneers is still far from being realized.

Below. The Harrier "jump jet," a V.T.O.L. aircraft, firing its rocket during a weapons exercise in America.

5: *Completing The Circle*

In the last chapter it was shown that the airman is gradually being replaced by technology. Air power is relying increasingly on guided missiles. The civil pilot and his colleague the air traffic controller are now supported by automation and computers. All this has had an unfortunate effect on the adventurous private airman.

Particularly in Europe, the skies are full of air traffic lanes along which civil aircraft are rigorously channelled. The consequent restrictions have seriously affected light aircraft, which have to be discouraged from crossing, or even flying close to, these traffic lanes. Only in countries that are highly developed and with great areas of open space, such as the United States and Australia, is the private flier free to travel where he likes. Even in these countries, the development of V.H.F. communications and automatic height reporting when picked up by radars, will increase the complexity and costs of private aviation.

In civil and military aviation, the development of electronic systems has led to a huge increase in the numbers of instruments to assist the pilot. The fault lies mainly with the pilots who, like many birds, are inveterate hoarders. Once an instrument has appeared on a panel, they feel unhappy without it. Yet, as systems multiply, the problem has to be solved.

It is now possible to provide the pilot with a television type of screen on which he can depict only those instruments in which he is interested. Such electronic displays are focused to infinity, and projected onto a glass screen in front of the pilot, so that the information he needs can be superimposed on the real world as seen through his own eyes. This is the well known "head-up" display.

The early pilot was a horseman, with a good seat and plenty of courage, mounted on a frisky machine. Today we have to ask whether the manager can be allowed to interfere with his

Below. A pilot using the "head-up display." He is turning the knobs on the selector panel to project the information he wants onto the glass screen in front of him.

Above. The aircraft of the future? Automation is making inherent stability less of a problem and aircraft may in time have no need of wings or fins.

systems provided they assure him that they are working properly. It is questionable whether the airman should be trained to take over in a variety of emergencies which are extremely unlikely to arise under any conditions.

As a result of automation the control column is becoming an anachronism in the civil and military aeroplane. Future aircraft may be flown not by strips of ironmongery that link human hands to elevators, ailerons and rudders, but by electronic nerves. In that event, inherent stability or handiness will not matter. The designer will be able to lop off stabilizing excrescences, such as fins, that tend to set up drag as they are driven through the air. Such flying machines will not be flyable by the pilot.

We have seen that aviation tends to be in conflict with the society that it serves, partly due to pollution by noise, and partly because modern airports compete with people and industry for large tracts of suburban land. Yet, air travel has its advantages. To travel abroad used to take so long that only a man of leisure could enjoy it fully. Now, the workers of the world with a week to spare, fly hundreds of miles to holiday resorts in specially chartered aeroplanes.

The early pioneers hoped that the aeroplane would bring nations closer together, just as the railways had linked up adjacent districts. Yet, in practice, it is television that has carried the frontiers of the world to our drawing rooms. Indeed, air travel has introduced great monotony. Whereas a seaport exhibits the character of the people who have developed it through the ages, airports all over the world are depressingly identical in shape and form.

Nor is it possible to see much of the world from a modern commercial aeroplane. With the jet aircraft has come a reduction in the size of the porthole to maintain the strength of the pressure cabin. In an aircraft such as the "Jumbo," with ten seats abreast, only the end occupants can peer out uncertainly at the Earth below. So the monotony of travel has to be mitigated by frequent meals and continuous radio or television shows.

The New Glory

Around 1927 a Society for Space was formed in Germany and work on rockets began. Other experiments were in progress in the United States but no rocketeer knew anything of the work outside his own country. In England, the Explosives Act of 1875 would have effectively discouraged any interest in rocketry.

Incredible risks were taken in the early pioneering days of rocketry. Progress became a matter of forgetting the dead quickly but remembering meticulously what had blown them up. In the early thirties, the son of a baron, Wernher von Braun (1912–   ), joined the group working in Germany. His shrewdness and his distinguished lineage endeared him to his Teutonic colleagues who were to form the team responsible for the *V2*, a vehicle which they regarded as far too good to be wasted by having to land on this planet.

The moment that the war was over, the Russians, Americans and British seized the German rocket technicians. Von Braun and some of his friends managed to elude their S.S. guards and gave themselves up to the United States Army. The others were mostly picked up by the Russians who, knowing little of the possibility of small atomic weapons, set them to work building huge rockets after the pattern of the hundred ton *V10*, which was already on the drawing board.

In 1957 the Russians astounded the world by launching the first space craft – unmanned Sputniks that orbitted the Earth. This success shocked the people of the United States. Von Braun and others were building long-range ballistic missiles and the Americans had a large fleet of manned atomic bombers, and yet here was Soviet ironmongery flying unhindered far above their heads. The propagandists were painting a picture of Russian backwardness while the USSR was forging ahead of the USA in the most highly technical field of all.

The Russians proceeded to rub salt into the wounds. In 1959 they sent an unmanned rocket to the Moon and two years later, after trials with dogs, Major Yuri Gagarin (1934–68) became the first astronaut. By then the President of the United States, John Kennedy (1917–63), had decided that America would land men on the Moon before the end of the 1960s. Already they had fired off a number of anaesthetized monkeys, each named Albert, which they found from telemetry suffered no ill effects until impact with the ground. In 1962 John Glenn (1921–   ) was successfully shot off into the sea like a human cannon ball, but a year later, the U.S.S.R. had a woman, Lieutenant

Below. One of the monkeys the Americans used to test the effects of weightlessness as part of their preparations for sending men to the Moon.

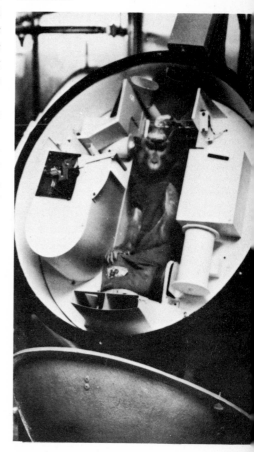

Tereshkova (1937–   ) orbitting the Earth.

The Russians were sending up crews wearing ordinary clothes inside fully pressurized capsules, who were breathing ordinary air. The Americans realized that it would take too long to develop the truly colossal launchers needed to carry men to the moon "in shirt sleeves." They decided to design capsules for crews working in an atmosphere of pure oxygen. In 1967, a dreadful disaster occurred. The oxygen, combining with unstable material, led to a fire inside a capsule undertaking a ground test, and three astronauts were burned to death. It was the fact that the tragedy occurred before the crew were even launched that shattered the confidence of the people in the United States.

But the Americans rallied with extraordinary courage. At the end of 1968 three astronauts circled the Moon and in July 1969 Neil Armstrong (1930–   ) and Edwin Aldrin (1930–   ) stepped out onto lunar dust. They had covered a quarter of a million miles and at times travelled at seven miles a second. The nation had achieved its objective within the time-scale stated publicly by President Kennedy in 1961. The world saw what courage, technical ability, good management and national willpower could accomplish. Von Braun's faith in rockets had been justified.

A huge sum of money had been spent on the Moon programme, a dozen times that devoted to producing the atomic bomb. New materials and new techniques had been introduced that were to pay handsome dividends in fields remote from space, and nobody can tell what will be the long-term benefits of the Moon landings and the later Sky-lab orbits. Yet, in one sense, the mission had not achieved its purpose. To the emerging nations of the world, space travel was too remote from their preoccupations with the immediate needs of their peoples. The prestige of the Americans depended far more on their performance on Earth.

And what of the astronauts? Selected with great care and highly trained for their specific roles, the gallant spacemen were in fact quite different from the usual pioneers. The first aviators were generally solitary souls in touch with nobody and were regarded as mad and subjected to ridicule. These new heroes were supported by huge teams of scientists and engineers, and on their voyages they were in constant touch with the ground and their every movement was known to controllers on Earth.

Yet even if their fantastic space effort failed to accomplish all that the United States had hoped, it still remains, like the Great Pyramid, the Acropolis and the ceiling of the Sistine Chapel, a monument for all time. Everybody on Earth is a little taller

Below. American astronaut on the Moon setting up a scientific experiment.

because man has walked on the Moon. In this sense, the American people were the true pioneers, criticized, even ridiculed but in the end triumphant. It was, as Armstrong said when he stepped on the Moon, "One great leap forward for mankind," some say the greatest of all.

Above. The control room at Houston where all the space flights are carefully monitored and a close watch is kept on the activities of the astronauts.

Pastimes

Man has made the necessities of the past into the pastimes of today. Hunting, shooting and fishing on which every man depended for life, are now expensive luxuries enjoyed by the privileged few. Two hundred years ago, people travelled about the country on foot or on horseback and today many people hike and ride for pleasure.

Although the glider disappeared when the aeroplane was born, it came to life again in Germany after World War I when that country was forbidden to build military aircraft. By the middle of the 1920s, German pilots were learning the arts of soaring and were keeping aloft on the "standing waves" caused by wind blowing up the faces of escarpments. Next they learned to use upcurrents in the air which occur due to local heating of the ground and to the instability of the atmosphere.

By such means, the Germans and Austrians learned to travel distances of up to a hundred miles and to climb many thousands of feet into the sky. Towards the end of the 1920s, soaring as a sport spread to Britain and America and, today, gliders are far more common sights than they have ever been before.

The glider itself has changed out of all recognition. To glide from one upcurrent to the next, the machine has to be able to travel the maximum distance with the minimum loss of height. As a result, the modern glider is a monoplane with very long narrow wings and the pilot is enclosed in a streamlined canopy, within a slender fuselage into which the single central undercarriage is retracted.

Not only has the glider reappeared but so has the hot air balloon. High energy burners used for camping can be used also to inflate balloons. To go up is then a matter of turning up the heater; to descend, the burner is cut back. These balloons are used mainly in temperate latitudes for, to provide lift in the tropics, the air would have to be heated to a temperature at which the fabric would disintegrate.

Ballooning is a sport that mixes motion, under conditions of quite extraordinary peace and quiet, with remarkable adventures on landing at the end of a virtually unplannable voyage. It is the antithesis of flight in the modern air traffic control environment. Nor has the sport been invaded by the circus element although balloons are occasionally used, like airships, for advertisements.

Below. One of the few airships which are used for advertising purposes. Recently there has been a great revival in ballooning in this country.

Even before the days of the balloon, man had sought to fly in the air like a bird. Today he has succeeded. Men and women have learned to direct themselves through the air by means of their arms and legs. "Sky divers" plummet out of aircraft and, when they reach a terminal velocity of around a hundred miles an hour, steer themselves about by means of their arms and legs. Already one foolhardy soul has thrown out his parachute, dived after it, caught it up and fitted it on, before landing safely.

Teams of skydivers steer themselves into patterns as they fall through the air. Wings are not fitted because, among other reasons, the force of the air could make it impossible for the hand to reach the parachute release. Thus man has come near to realizing his oldest dream – to fly through the air with his arms as wings. The circle started in mythology by Icarus has been completed.

Above. Skydivers steering themselves about the skies—the nearest man has come to flying through the air with his arms as wings.

Glossary

AEROFOIL. A surface that reacts to the slip-stream due to motion through the air.

AILERON. An aerofoil in the wing of an aeroplane used to control the craft in roll.

AIR TRAFFIC CONTROL. A ground organization whose main aim is to prevent air collisions.

AIRSCREW. A propeller used in an aeroplane.

AIRSHIP. A lighter-than-air craft that can move under its own power. Sometimes known as a dirigible.

AIRSPEED INDICATOR. An instrument that provides warning of a stall.

ALTIMETER. An instrument that provides an indication of height above mean sea level.

AMPHIBIAN. An aircraft that can take off from either water or land.

ARTIFICIAL HORIZON. An instrument that shows a pilot the attitude of his craft.

ATTITUDE. The tilt of an aircraft fore and aft or sideways compared to the vertical.

AUTOGYRO. Correctly a trade name but applied generally to all aircraft with freely rotating wings.

BIPLANE. An aircraft whose lift is derived from two fixed-wings one above the other.

CONTROL COLUMN. A device that operates ailerons and elevators manually.

DELTA. A dart shaped wing.

DIHEDRAL. A wing whose roots are lower than its tips.

DIRIGIBLE. The original term for an airship.

DROOP. A retractable aerofoil fitted to the leading edge of a wing.

ELEVATOR. An aerofoil usually in the tail of an aeroplane to control the craft fore and aft.

FLAP. A retractable aerofoil fitted to the trailing edge of a wing.

FLYING BOAT. An aeroplane with a hull that can float on the water and allow for take-off or landing.

GIROPLANE. American name for an autogyro.

GLIDER. An unpowered aeroplane. A high performance glider is known as a sailplane.

HELICOPTER. An aircraft in which lift is provided by rotating the wings. Also known in America as a rotorcraft.

I.L.S. A precise approach and landing system.

INERTIAL NAVIGATION. Automatic navigation and attitude information depending on gyroscopes and accelerometers.

LIFT. The force exerted by an aerofoil in the direction opposite to gravity.

MONOPLANE. An aircraft whose lift is derived from a single wing.

NACELLE. A unit in which a power plant is installed.

ORTHINOPTER. A device that flies by flapping wings.

PEDESTAL. A mounting for controls sited between the two pilots' seats in a civil or military aircraft.

PROPELLER. A rotary device that generates airflow. Also known in aircraft as an airscrew.

RADAR. A radio system that measures distances and directions of objects simultaneously. The information is generally presented as a map on a screen.

RIP CORD. The device that operates a parachute.

ROCKET. A motor that generates thrust by means of its self-contained propellant and needs no oxygen from the air.

ROTORCRAFT. American name for helicopter.

RUDDER. An aerofoil surface that turns a craft to left or right.

SAILPLANE. A high performance glider.

SEAPLANE. An aeroplane that lands and takes-off on the water using floats.

SKYDIVER. A parachutist who manoeuvres himself in the air by means of his arms and legs before pulling the rip cord.

STALL. Sudden loss of lift in a wing due to inadequate air flow.

STICK. An elementary control column.

S.T.O.L. Short take-off and landing aircraft.

TELEMETRY. The relaying of instrument readings usually by radio devices.

TURBO-JET. A jet engine in which the air is sucked into the front end by a fan. Sometimes known as a turbo-fan in the United States.

UNDERCARRIAGE. The system that supports an aircraft on the ground.

V.O.R. A beacon which an aircraft can approach or leave along a chosen path.

V.T.O.L. Vertical take-off and landing aircraft.

Date Chart

AD

1452–1519	Leonardo da Vinci designs orthinopter and parachute.
1783	First balloon flown by Montgolfier brothers.
1797	Garnerin makes first parachute descent.
1842	Henson patents his *aerial steam carriage* which will not fly.
1804–1853	Cayley flies gliders.
1870	Balloons lift people and letters from beseiged Paris.
1891	Lilienthal killed in a "hang-glider."
1901	Santos Dumont flies his airship around the Eiffel Tower.
1903	Wright brothers' first flight in aeroplane.
1908	Bleriot crosses the English Channel.
1915	Zeppelins bomb London.
1919	Alcock and Brown fly non-stop across the Atlantic.
1927	Lindbergh flies solo from New York to Paris.
1930	Amy Johnson flies to Australia from England in a Moth.
1931	Francis Chichester crosses the Tasman sea.
1940	Battle of Britain.
1944	V weapons launched by Germany.
1945	Atomic bombs dropped on Japan.
1952	First jet aircraft in commercial service, the Comet, subsequently withdrawn 1954–8.
1958	Jet transports appear in Britain, United States and France.
1961	Gagarin, the first man in space.
1969	Americans land on the Moon. First Jumbo jets appear.
1975?	Supersonic aircraft in service.

This book belongs to:

....

AESOP'S FABLES

PUBLISHED BY PETER HADDOCK LIMITED,
BRIDLINGTON, ENGLAND
PRINTED IN ITALY

ISBN 07105 0246 X

The Sleeping Dog

Every night the Hunter, who lived in the forest, left his dog outside to guard the house. This was a very good arrangement, especially for the dog, who instead of guarding the house, always fell asleep and had wonderful dreams.
He dreamt of all the pleasant things in a dog's life, especially food — chicken legs, joints of lamb and many other delicious meals.

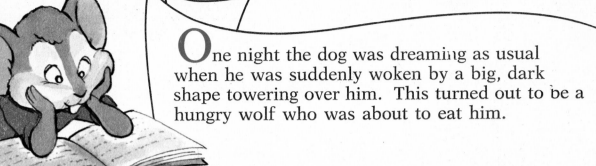

One night the dog was dreaming as usual when he was suddenly woken by a big, dark shape towering over him. This turned out to be a hungry wolf who was about to eat him.

Very quickly, the dog had an idea to save himself. He pointed out to the wolf that he was very thin and hardly worth eating. However, he was due to be fed a large meal which would make him much fatter and a better meal for the wolf. The wolf, being very greedy, said he would come back the next night.

As soon as the wolf left, the dog barked furiously and woke his master who dressed quickly and came out of the house to investigate the noise. By this time it was daylight and the Hunter found the tracks left by the wolf.

The Hunter was pleased with his dog as he believed the dog's actions had saved his chickens, several of which had been stolen recently. As a reward he fed the dog very well and decided he could sleep indoors provided the wolf did not steal any more chickens.

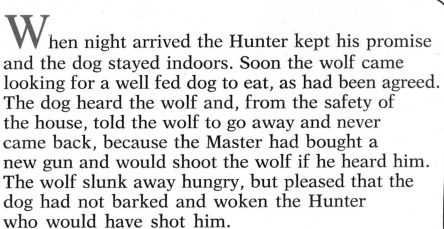

When night arrived the Hunter kept his promise and the dog stayed indoors. Soon the wolf came looking for a well fed dog to eat, as had been agreed. The dog heard the wolf and, from the safety of the house, told the wolf to go away and never came back, because the Master had bought a new gun and would shoot the wolf if he heard him. The wolf slunk away hungry, but pleased that the dog had not barked and woken the Hunter who would have shot him.

The Fox and the Woodcutter

There once was a fox who never raided farmers' chicken huts nor killed their ducks. The farmers knew this and left the fox alone. One day, two hunters saw the fox and immediately tried to kill him. Luckily the fox had seen the danger and ran away very swiftly but the hunters followed.

As soon as they reached the best pastures, the wild goats took to their heels and ran down a steep, rocky ravine. The goatherd could not follow but shouted for them to come back.

The wild goats replied that they preferred their freedom and hunger to being kept in a dark stable for days knowing that they would end up at the market.

The Donkey and the Dog

man owned a donkey and a dog but treated the two animals differently. The dog received good food and plenty of attention whilst the donkey had to work hard all day long bringing loads of firewood to the house and only being fed hay. He was not allowed in the house but had to sleep in a stable.

The donkey grew tired of all this and asked the dog why their master treated them differently. The dog thought about this and told the donkey that he was always very friendly to their master, wagging his tail and jumping up and down when he met him. Sometimes he even licked his masters hands.

The next day when the master came for the donkey he got a surprise. The donkey jumped up and down, grabbed his master and licked his face with his great, long tongue. The donkey was, of course, much bigger than the dog and the master was almost knocked over. He thought the donkey had gone mad.

The master was so annoyed at the donkey's stupid behaviour that he picked up a stick and gave him a good beating. The poor donkey moaned to the dog that it seemed once a donkey always a donkey, especially if his embraces were mistaken for kicks. It seemed there was no way for him to change his way of life.